Dangerous Enthusiasms

Dangerous Enthusiasms

E-government, Computer Failure and Information System Development

ROBIN GAULD & SHAUN GOLDFINCH

WITH TONY DALE

OTAGO

Published by Otago University Press
PO Box 56/Level 1, 398 Cumberland Street, Dunedin, New Zealand
Fax: 64 3 479 8385. Email: university.press@otago.ac.nz

First published 2006

ISBN-13: 978 1 877372 34 6
ISBN-10: 1 877372 34 x

Cover Image: U.S. Army Photo, from the archives of the
ARL Technical Library.

Printed by Astra Print Ltd, Wellington

Contents

Acknowledgements

We are grateful to:

the State Services Commission and LINZ for providing access to their archives and photocopying service, and to LINZ for their detailed comments on the Landonline chapter;
the various consultants and public servants who agreed to be interviewed;
Ray Delany for providing Figure 3.1 in chapter 3;
Stuart Barson for assisting with the research that underpins chapter 4;
Tony Dale for helping to produce an earlier version of the INCIS chapter and his assistance with other aspects of this book;
Otago University Press for supporting this project and seeing it through to print;
Andrew Parsloe for producing the index;
the University of Otago for funding the New Zealand Health Sector Transition Project, under the auspices of which some of the research in chapters 3 and 4 was conducted;
Ina Bercinskas, Ted Bercinskas-Gauld and Honor Bercinskas-Gauld for moral support.

The responsibility for any errors and omissions remains, of course, with us.

Robin Gauld & Shaun Goldfinch
May 2006

Abbreviations used in text

ADT	Admission, Discharge and Transfer
AHB	Area Health Board
CCH	Capital Coast Health Limited
CCMAU	Crown Company Monitoring Advisory Unit
CHE	Crown Health Enterprise
CR1	Core Records System 1
CR2	Core Records System 2
DHB	District Health Board
EHN	electronic health network
EMR	Electronic Medical Record
HFA	Health Funding Authority
HW	Health Waikato Ltd
ICT	information and computer technology
IS	information system
ISD	information system development
IT	information technology
INCIS	Integrated National Crime Investigation System
JUG	joined-up government
LINZ	Land Information New Zealand
MH	Mental Health
NHI	National Health Index
NIIPS	National Information Infrastructure Protection Strategy
NMDS	National Minimum Data Set
NPI	National Provider Index
NPR	National Performance Review
NPV	Net Present Value
NPM	New Public Management
NZHIS	New Zealand Health Information Service
OECD	Organisation of Economic Cooperation and Development
PACS	Picture Archiving and Communication System
PwC	PricewaterhouseCoopers
RFI	Request for Information
RFT	Request for Tender
RHA	Regional Health Authority
ROC	Review of the Centre
SEE	Secure Electronic Environment
SMS	Shared Medical Systems

1.

E-government and Information System Development

Governments have always been concerned with the collection, management, use and dissemination of information – together these are a key ingredient of decision- and policy-making; indeed, of the very act of governing. Information systems have evolved from vast paper archives, to communications by various postal systems, to incorporate telegraph, then telephone, telex, and fax. In the latter part of the twentieth century, computers began to play a central role in society and government. Initially, these were stand-alone mainframes dedicated to data storage. From the 1980s, personal computers began arriving on the desks of public servants, becoming increasingly ubiquitous at the same time as they grew in sophistication and power.

The last two decades have seen the emergence of the internet, the world-wide-web and networked computing, spawning vast new sources of information, new communities, new types of communication and social interaction, and even new languages. Governments across the world have eagerly embraced these new technologies. Many have issued ambitious 'electronic-government' (henceforth e-government) strategies bringing information and computer technology (ICT) to the centre of government. Underlying many e-government initiatives is the assumption that they will 'reinvent' the ways in which governments are structured, how they are managed and how they interact with the wider community.

'E-government' is a multifaceted concept, with different meanings appealing to different constituents. We suspect this explains much of its allure. For politicians, e-government may simply be a useful rhetorical device into which various reform strategies can be bundled. On the one hand, it fits well into the managerial mode, with claims of improved efficiency and government 're-engineering'. However, along with claims of enhanced service and public engagement, it also offers much for those seeking to calm a public dissatisfied with managerialism, or new public management (NPM).[1] For those leading or employed in government agencies, ICT may be viewed as a managerial tool, to assist in making the administration of government work more efficient by acting as a cost-cutting device for reducing and streamlining levels of information exchange and service delivery. Indeed, e-government may simply be a new and more acceptable face behind which managerialism can allow its objectives to be further advanced. For the public and various interest groups, and some scholars, the new information technologies are regarded as sources of greater information about, and influence over, government; indeed, as a way of facilitating greater participatory and grass-roots-type democracy.

In this book, we sound a somewhat cautious note when it comes to e-government and information technology generally. Despite the often unabashed enthusiasm for information technology found across the public and private spheres, the hope for better service and improved, streamlined administration, and the fuel ICT provides for sometimes excited political rhetoric, ICT needs to be approached carefully. As we will point out (drawing on case studies in New Zealand as well as a growing body of international research), even when technically successful, ICT projects do not often deliver the financial and other benefits they promise. It is the remarkable ubiquity of the failure of ICT projects – particularly large ICT projects – and the large sums of money that can disappear as a result that should be of most concern: however, this is not often the case. In the face of a continued enthusiasm for ICT despite the pervasive failure that has persisted for decades, we argue for a pessimism in information system development.

Failure of large and complex information system developments (ISDs) is largely unavoidable. Even systems that work in a technical sense often do not deliver all that is expected of them. This is not a problem simply to be solved by a new management, reporting or software engineering technique or some other silver bullet, as much of the literature from the management and IT professions suggests. Rather, the central problem is the overblown and unrealistic expectations that many people have regarding information technology. In this chapter, a model of the four enthusiasms that encourages these overblown expectations is outlined. Once begun, highly complex projects are extremely difficult to monitor and control, and prevent from failing. When projects fail, it is difficult to find and hold to account those responsible. Consequently, investments in technology should be approached with great caution in the public sector, and complex and large developments in information technology, particularly if new technology is involved, should be avoided if at all possible. Investments, if they are to be made, should have modest aims and use proven technology. In many cases, it may be better to avoid an investment altogether and continue with existing systems, at least until the technology improves.

ICT Failure and Success in the Public Sector

There are ICT and e-government success stories. These tend to be smaller projects, often initiated from the bottom up. New Zealand medical general practitioner networks, formed through the 1990s and often with several hundred members across multiple practice sites, receive state subsidies for various services and must also collect and provide patient data to the government. Today, most practitioner networks have highly sophisticated information systems of world-class standard. Similarly, the Counties Manukau District Health Board's information system, development of which commenced in the mid-1990s, facilitates a sophisticated array of information-sharing mechanisms between hospitals, community-based general practitioners and pharmacies in the area (Brimacombe 2003). Again, this is a world-leading initiative.

But success is not the norm in computer developments. Indeed, the great majority of information system developments are unsuccessful. The larger the development, the more likely it will be unsuccessful. While exact numbers are uncertain, and depend to some extent on how success is measured, something like 20 to 30 per cent of developments are total failures, with projects abandoned. Around 30 to 60 per cent are partial failures, involving time and cost overruns and/or other problems. The minority are those counted as successes (Collins and Bicknell 1997; Corner and Hinton 2002; Georgiadou 2003; Heeks, Mundy, and Salazar 1999; Heeks 2002; Iacovou 1999; James 1997; Korac-Boisvert and Kouzmin 1995; Royal Academy of Engineering and British Computer Society 2004; Standish Group 2001; 2004).

In a US survey of IS projects by the Standish Group, it was found that success rates varied from 59 per cent in the retail sector, to 32 per cent in the financial sector, to 27 per cent in manufacturing, and 18 per cent in government. Overall, the success rate was 26 per cent. Forty-six per cent of projects had problems including being over budget and behind schedule, or being delivered with fewer functions and features than originally specified. Twenty-eight per cent failed altogether or were cancelled. Cost overruns averaged nearly 200 per cent. This success rate varied dramatically by total project budget: at less than US$750,000 the success rate was 55 per cent; with budgets over $10 million, no project was successful (SIMPL/NZIER 2000). More recent Standish Group (2004) estimates saw success rates at 29 per cent, problems with 53 per cent of projects, and an 18 per cent failure rate. The Royal Academy of Engineering and the British Computer Society (2004) found that 84 per cent of public sector ICT projects resulted in failure of some sort.

New Zealand has had its share of public sector ICT problems. Recent failures include a Health Waikato project, abandoned at the cost of NZ$17 million, and the failure of a large part of a NZ$26 million project by Capital Coast Health (see Chapters 3 and 4). Archives New Zealand's $7 million project to create an online index of its holdings faced continual delays. The Department of Child, Youth and Family Service's $12.7 million Cyras computer system was introduced in 2000, late and with limited functionality and significant and continuing problems. The 'department had to appoint 40 staff as fulltime "expert users" for four months, at unknown cost, to help their colleagues use the computer system' (Milne 2002). In 2003 the Parliamentary Counsel Office's $8.2 million PAL system was reviewed after the main contractor, UNISYS, 'requested financial assurances before completing the project' to cover 'extra work, over and above the project's original specifications' (Bell 2003). The Department of Courts' $32 million computerisation initiative ran at least $8 million over budget. The Ministry of Social Development's troubled SWIFTT project faced continued media and political interest. A New Zealand Government study in 2000 found 38 per cent of government projects were judged a success, 59 per cent involved problems, and 3 per cent were judged a complete failure or were cancelled. Government success rates were slightly higher than private sector success rates, at 31 per cent. At over the NZ$10 million mark, however, the success rate for both was zero (SIMPL/NZIER 2000).

The sums involved can be staggering. A study of ISDs in the British public sector estimated that 20 per cent of expenditure was wasted, while a further 30 to 40 per cent led to no perceivable benefits (Wilcocks 1994). In 1994, the US General Accounting Office reported that the spending of over $200 billion in the previous twelve years had led to few meaningful returns. Collins and Bicknell (1997) estimated public sector failures in the UK cost £5 billion. For example, the UK's public health service Resource Management Initiative led to new information systems being introduced into almost every hospital. Despite the expenditure of hundreds of millions of pounds, few were successful 'by any criteria' (Heeks and Bhatnagar 1999: 59). The Wessex Health Authority's Regional Information Systems Plan was cancelled after something between £43 million and £60 million (the actual figure was uncertain) had already been spent, with almost nothing achieved (Collins and Bicknell 1997). A benefit payment scheme, involving the British Post Office, the Department of Social Security and the computer company ICL, was abandoned after three years at the cost of £300 million (*Economist* 2002). An already obsolete air-traffic support system opened in Swanson, UK, in 2002, six years late and £180 million over budget (*Economist* 2002).

Vast sums of money, mostly provided by aid agencies, have been spent on health and other information systems in South Africa, on donor-funded IS projects in China, and on World Bank funded projects in Africa – nearly all of which have been total or partial failures (Heeks 2002). The Canadian Firearms Program blew out from initial estimates of Can$113 million to over $1 billion, an overrun of almost 900 per cent (Auditor General of Canada 2002). Spectacularly, the US Internal Revenue Service, with an annual computer budget of $8 billion, managed 'a string of project failures that have cost taxpayers $50 billion a year [mainly defined as revenue forgone] – roughly as much as the yearly net profit of the entire computer industry' (James 1997: 1). It is estimated that across both the public and private sectors, around $US150 billion is wasted per annum on ICT failures in the United States and $US140 billion in the European Union (Dalcher and Genus 2003). Despite the catalogue of continuing failures, and despite decades of attempts to deal with the problem, there is little evidence that ISD failures are decreasing in the public sector.

Governments continue to commission ambitious large-scale projects. The world's largest-ever public-sector project commenced in 2002 at an estimated cost of US$11 billion. It aims to create an information system for the United Kingdom's National

Health Service. If successful, the system will allow, amongst others things, electronic transmission of prescriptions, online booking of hospital services from remote locations, and portable electronic patient records. Initial troubles led to suggestions it may never deliver on planned aims. It may be that, with a decade-long timetable to completion, it is 'too early' to tell whether failure will occur (*Economist* 2004). However, given the research drawn upon in this book, the probability of failure is very large indeed.

What is ICT Failure?

Failure is a social construct and perceptions of what is and is not failure can vary between persons, and over time (Bovens and 't Hart 1996). Opinions differ as to what extent failure is a normal part of public policy – or whether it is an unusual, if sometimes spectacular, event seized on by the media for the sake of eye-catching headlines (Bovens, 't Hart and Peters 2001). What distinguishes IS failure from other failures in the public sector, however, is its overwhelming ubiquity. Indeed, while some writers might claim failure in IS development is overstated, the bulk of the research suggests failure might even be the norm. As Mahaney and Lederer (1999: 291) note, 'because this problem has endured for three decades, many IS professionals have accepted failure as inevitable'.

Bascarini (1999) notes 'a standardized definition of project success does not exist, nor [is there] an accepted methodology for measuring it'. Indeed, what is counted as failure 'depends on who you ask' and perceptions of success and failure may change over time (Larsen and Myers 1999). The Standish Group sees success in narrow terms, namely if a project is delivered on time and on budget, with functions and features delivered as originally specified. KPMG has defined 'runaway projects' to be those that overrun their projected budget or completion date by more than 30 per cent, while others have proposed an overrun on budget or timeframe of 100 per cent as a measure of failure (Cole 1995; Glass 1998). However, failure does not necessarily imply only technical failure – that is, even if a system performs as its designers intend, it may not be used as intended, or used at all, and so still be considered a failure (Laudon and Laudon 1998; Dutton et al. 1995). Even projects that meet design specifications may not increase worker productivity or deliver other expected gains – productivity may even decrease. Indeed, there has been considerable debate regarding productivity and other benefits of IS in the last three decades, in both the public and private sectors and in the economy generally (Coltman et al. 2001; Norris and Moon 2005; Northrop et al. 1990; Hewson and Hewson 1998). Benefits may not offset the costs of development; indeed, a long project can cause years of serious and costly disruption to operations that may never be recovered (Norris and Moon 2005; Teega Associates Ltd 2003). Alternatively – despite technical flaws such as project overruns, over-spending, design questions and so on – some systems may be deemed a success (Wilson and Howcroft 2002).

Similarly, a project may be considered a failure, but later be re-evaluated as a success for reasons quite outside the technical success of the project (Huang et al. 2003).

Drawing on Wilson and Howcroft (2002: 237), a number of types of failure can be summarised:

> (1) Project failure. The project does not meet the agreed standards, including the functions provided, budget, or completion deadlines
>
> (2) System failure. The system does not work properly, including not performing as expected, not being operational at the specified time or not being used in the way intended. Even when used as intended, the project may not generate productivity gains or deliver the benefits expected.
>
> (3) User failure. The system is not used because of user resistance, due to such things as recalcitrance, lack of staff training and ability, and the complexity of the new system.

Why do Information System Projects Fail?

The considerable literature on the causes of IS failure, and the solution to this ongoing problem, largely reflects the latest management fad. None of these fads has been particularly successful in preventing failures, and most have soon been abandoned for new solutions. Of the more promising, Heeks has proposed a checklist of 'Critical Failure Factors' (Heeks 1999; Heeks and Bhatnagar 1999). These include data inadequacies; technical problems; management, process and technical skill shortages; cultural clashes and political infighting; and external environmental factors (Table 1.1). While useful, a factor approach is critiqued by a number of writers. First, 'the factor approach tends to view implementation as a static process instead of a dynamic phenomenon, and ignores the potential for a factor to have varying levels of importance at different stages of the implementation process' (Larsen and Myers 1999). Second, the relationship between the factors is often unexplained (Ginzberg 1981; Lucas 1981). Indeed, the approach can assume that each factor is an independent variable and thus underplays the interaction between them (Nandhakumar 1996; Bussen and Myers 1997). Third, a number of studies have shown a lack of consistency in the importance of factors, and few factors have been important in all cases (Kwon and Zmud 1987). Fourth, the factor approach is claimed, perhaps unfairly, to be overly mechanist while underplaying the importance of such things as organisational culture in development and the importance of the political, social and environmental context within and outside the organisation (Nandhakumar 1996; Bussen and Myers 1997). This last criticism would be difficult to sustain in relation to Heek's critical factor approach, which explicitly takes account of such environmental, cultural, and political factors. Finally, the critical failure factor, while possibly useful in explaining in retrospect why failure may have occurred, provides little guidance on how to avoid it. Indeed, if anything, the approach highlights the remarkable complexity of ISDs, the myriad problems that can occur, and the difficulty that exists in addressing them. And it does not adequately address why large projects continue to be initiated, a question we discuss below.

More recently, IS failure has been seen as a problem of learning, where organisations fail to learn from external and internal sources, and fail to moderate beliefs and behaviour in the face of failure. This behaviour includes persisting in IS developments long after they have proved to be unfeasible (Irani, Sharif, and Love 2001; Lyytinen and Robey 1999; Wastell 1999). Organisations fail to learn, it is claimed, because of the limits imposed by such things as information overload, high turnover of skilled staff, embedded ways of thinking, the drawing of strong conclusions from limited individual experiences, and an inability (and lack of incentives) to draw lessons from previous failures (which are often forgotten) (Lyytinen and Robey 1999). The separation of IS from other units within a business, and its overwhelming technological and engineering background, can also isolate IT specialists from wider issues and learning. Over time, it is claimed, organisations 'accept and expect poor performance while creating organizational myths that perpetuate short-term optimization' (Lyytinen and Robey 1999: 85). The high levels

Factor	Description	Factor	Description
Cultural	Clashes with national/local culture	*Process*	Processes are inadequate to integrate community or channel relevant information
Environmental	Factors outside the organisation disrupt project		
Information	Information and data inadequacies	*Strategic*	IS not coordinated across different agencies or divisions
Management	Lack of management skills, knowledge and training	*Structural*	IS clashes with organisational and/or management structures
People	Lack of staff with sufficient training, skills or inclination to handle or develop IT	*Technical*	Problems with IT such as incompatibility across agencies
Political	Political infighting derails project		

Table 1.1. Critical Failure Factors in IS Disasters
Source: Heeks and Bhantnagar (1999).

of stress and anxiety involved for participants in IS projects also undermine learning (Wastell 1999). Groups and individuals cope with this stress through 'defence-avoidance behavior patterns' such as reliance on organisational ritual, political infighting, and isolationism where groups develop a 'laager' mentality and an inward-looking, mutually supporting and outwardly suspicious 'groupthink' ('t Hart 1994). These defences enable people to avoid having to engage with the problems in the project, and face up to and learn from these problems (Wastell 1999). Failure then, it is claimed, will be reduced by creating incentives for organisations and individuals to learn, such as rewarding bearers of bad news and mistakes, providing a supportive environment for learning, integrating IS within the wider organisation, and a broader focus of IS developers away from their mainly technical focus (Lyytinen and Robey 1999; Wastell 1999).

While it provides some insights, the 'learning organisation' has been seen as having questionable empirical foundations (Salaman 2001). It is unclear as to what learning actually is and who (the organisation or the individual) is carrying out the learning (and sometimes the two are conflated) (Popper and Lipshitz 2000). The 'learning organisation' underplays the barriers that exist to learning due to the strong culture, hierarchy, and rituals of organisations, and the 'paradigm', 'discourse' or belief systems (mostly external to the organisation) within which managers work and which rule out some options and constrain others (Salaman 2001). As March and Olsen (1996) argue, there are certain things that can be done and not done – a certain 'logic of appropriateness' that can provide barriers to learning.

The question also arises how useful some of the 'learning organisation' literature is in explaining IS failures, particularly in the public sector. First, the continued high level of IS failures shows there is little evidence that learning occurs now or that it will in the future. Second, it is unclear what the organisation should learn in order to avoid IS failure. There is no agreement on what software development methodologies or latest management system or template is effective. None has been particularly successful so far. A number of critics note how management is characterised by the adoption of 'fads', in which popularity has little to do with actual evidence of effectiveness; how the fad is usually abandoned after a few years in the face of less than fantastic results, and a new fad is embraced equally as enthusiastically (Brindle and Stearns 2001; Birnum 2000). Systems for government information technology management show some of the same tendencies (Holden 2003). Software development is similarly afflicted. As Georgiadou (2003: 125) notes:

> Researchers and practitioners endeavoured to find ways of improving the productivity and quality of products. New languages were often believed to have almost magical powers of getting over the crisis. Automated tools, formal methods and, more recently, the object-orientated approach were proposed as alternative "religions" for Software Engineers becoming ardent followers of one approach or another.

Computer science, information systems, and software engineering created a large number of lifecycle models, methodologies, and metrics designed for solving problems of quality of both software products and software processes. Unfortunately... few of them were subjected to careful experimentation and were often adopted with limited empirical evidence of their correctness or effectiveness (Georgiadou 2003: 139).

Despite decades of development, there are still no reliable methods of estimating software project size or costs, and no software development methodology that guarantees good results (Georgiadou 2003). Software estimation is still reliant on the judgement of skilled individuals for success, and even the best can be wrong (Evans 2001). Fenton (1997) found experienced managers were over 50 per cent wrong in estimating software costs, and some software tools produced results that were incorrect by 200 per cent. This was for completely specified projects, using experienced people and well-proven technology. Jacobson, Rumbaugh, and Booch (1998: 354) found estimated project size at the beginning of a project 'may differ from the final size by a substantial percentage, say 50 per cent.'

Third, the learning literature focuses on IS within a firm or an organisation, and integrating that IS division or section into the wider needs of the organisation. However, government agencies are often dependent on external consultants to advise on IS developments, and for large IT companies to develop and supply software and hardware. Failure might encourage learning, but not necessarily a type of learning that will greatly benefit the purchaser. A consultancy company might learn that advising to proceed with a large IS project guarantees a flow of income in the future (quite apart from the value of this IS project to the purchaser) and with little risk that poor quality advice will affect financial rewards then and in the future. IT companies and their sales staff might learn that promising largely unachievable results from highly expensive IS projects is a good way to subsidise their software and hardware research and increase company profits – with little risk that contracts, however many pages they might run to, will be able to hold them to account. There is little evidence that consultants, IT companies, and public agencies, or many practitioners and academics, have learnt one of the key lessons of IS failure – that large and ambitious projects should be treated with great caution or avoided altogether.

The Four Enthusiasms of ICT Failure

Despite decades of failure, enthusiasm for large and complex investments in IS continues unabated, with 'e-government' presently heading the charge. To explain why large and ambitious projects continue to be initiated, we propose a model containing four pathological enthusiasms. Each enthusiasm is linked to a key player or group within public sector ISDs. The first is 'idolisation' or 'technological infatuation', where politicians and public officials 'use computers and are over-aware of IT's potential. They believe that IT can transform the business of government. The public sector becomes awash with IT-driven reform projects, which place technology at the heart of the change process' (Heeks and Bhatnagar 1999: 27). Indeed, public servants can be 'carried away' with the excitement of it all, providing reports and projections about the benefits of new developments that verge on the fantastic (Dale and Goldfinch 2002).

The second is technophilia or 'the myth of the technological fix', where 'the entire IS profession perpetuates the myth that better technology, and more of it, are the remedies for practical problems' (Lyytinen and Robey 1999: 95). Many who enter the IT industries are, in common parlance, 'geeks': they are 'enthusiasts' for computers and technology, excited by the possibilities new technologies offer and by the challenging intellectual puzzles that developing new technology brings. Technological development can become an end in itself. And as noted, programmers are also subject to bouts of enthusiasm for the new programming methodologies that come along every few years, again despite little evidence of their efficacy (Georgiadou 2003).

The third, 'lomanism', draws on Arthur Miller's archetypal salesman, Willie Loman, in *Death of a Salesman*. Lomanism is the enthusiasm, feigned or genuine, that sales representatives and other employees develop for their company's products and skills, and that company's ability to develop new products and technologies, whatever the objections or questions put forward by potential and actual purchasers and others involved in purchasing and developing the technology. IT salespersons can be faced by an unusually responsive audience; often those involved in finally deciding on what systems to buy are those responsible for promoting new developments in the first place. Those salespersons or company employees with the temerity to suggest purchasers' expectations might be somewhat overblown are likely to find purchasers will simply go to a company that promises their expectations will be met.

Fourth, there is 'managerial faddism'. This is the tendency for consultants and managers to eagerly embrace the newest management fad, methodology or utterings of the management guru of the moment and to see problems as largely solvable (or preventable) through better or more 'rational' management, and the appointment of skilled managers. Such managerial faddism is also reflected in the belief that most problems can be fixed or prevented, and benefits created, by improving management structures along the lines of the new fad, with new IS projects often being a key element. The orthodoxy of new public management (NPM) that has taken hold in New Zealand and across the world – its inherent belief in the supremacy of the private over the public sector, and its innovative, 'entrepreneurial' focus – provides a ready ground for such faddism. The public sector must now compete with the private in terms of its adoption of new technologies, including management ones, or face being seen as behind the times and resistant to change. Indeed, one of the benefits of pre-NPM Weberian (bureaucratic) models of public administration may have been lost – the much maligned preference for precedent, stability, and tradition (du Gay 2000).

Together these four enthusiasms feed off and mutually reinforce each other, in a vicious cycle, creating a strongly held belief that new and large IS projects will be a good idea. Doubters and sceptics can be portrayed as 'negative', 'not team players', 'not helpful' or, particularly in a public sector influenced by new public management and economic models of behaviour such as public choice, as 'vested' or 'rent-seeking' interest groups. Together these pathologies make up the 'Four Enthusiasms of IT Failure' (Figure 1.1). When a project enters difficulties, these four enthusiasms can also undermine attempts to curtail or abandon it – a project can always be fixed with better management, or more technology, hardware or better programming – or just a reassuring 'it'll be right on the night'.

Problems of Control

Rational models of management and decision-making seek to impose order and control on a complex and turbulent world that (it is believed) can be more or less understood (Brown and Brudney 2003; Lindblom 1988 [1959]). However, rather than showing aspects of 'linear logic', where cause and effect are known and can be controlled, ISDs show aspects of complex systems where the 'ability to predict the course of events is limited' and where even small events can lead to unpredictable outcomes (Turner 1998: 1). Much of the writing on ISD and IS failure suffers from a hubristic belief that once the correct information is available, the right management system and programming methodology adopted, and rational optimising individuals given the right incentives, the problem of failure will largely be solved. In contrast, we argue that due to problems of agency, immense complexity, and the interaction of human beings of, at best, only bounded or even

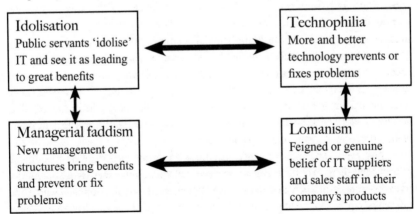

Figure 1.1. The Four Enthusiasms of ICT Failure

limited rationality, it is difficult to understand and control large ISDs. It is difficult to monitor and be aware of problems, to find solutions to these problems and hold to account those responsible for the failures. The sheer complexity of ISDs means humans, whose abilities are not unlimited, are faced with informational overload. Public agencies also work within a sometimes unstable legislative environment, with computer requirements subject to change in the face of changing laws, which further increases the complexity and cost (Small 2000). These issues are expanded on below.

Problems of Agency and Information

Problems of agency in ISDs can be considerable. Agency theory focuses on the problems faced by the principal (such as the manager or chief executive) in controlling an optimising agent (such as a programmer or IS developer and project manager) in a situation of information asymmetry and problems of monitoring where the agent may have greater knowledge of problems and an incentive to conceal them. In many cases, reliable information is simply not available on the actual progress of projects (as opposed to reported progress) due to the intangible nature of software development, the often dynamic and changeable nature of the project itself, the large number of diverse participants involved in the project (who may well be working in different parts of the world), and the sheer complexity and information overload faced in a large project (Smith, Keil, and Depledge 2001). Reflecting this, progress and audit reports are, in many cases, largely exercises in hope and fantasy (Dale and Goldfinch 2002).

Problems may not be made known to management or monitoring agencies. That members of organisations are reluctant to be bearers of bad news is a well-reported phenomenon (Tesser and Rosen 1972). IS developments are no different, with bad news often under-reported, concealed, and sometimes falsified (Collins and Bicknell 1997; Dale and Goldfinch 2002; Heeks and Bhatnagar 1999; Smith, Keil, and Depledge 2001). At times, public agencies have been reluctant to give information to monitoring agencies because of claims of 'commercial sensitivity' (Small 2000). Even if bad news is reported, it may not be listened to; indeed, bearers of bad news can suffer sanctions themselves (Keil and Robey 2001). Where a senior manager or chief executive is tightly linked to the project and identified with its success, he or she can be reluctant to admit to bad news or to curtail the project in the face of difficulties (Collins and Bicknell 1997; Dale and Goldfinch 2002; Heeks and Bhatnagar 1999; Keil and Robey 2001; Smith, Keil, and Depledge 2001).

In any event, line managers may not have the experience required to evaluate projects and there may be a tension between authority from expertise and authority from position, particularly in a highly complex field such as IS development where line managers may be supervising people with highly specialist skills, which these managers do not necessarily understand (Beetham 1996). Appointment in bureaucracies is often made on seniority and successful political behaviour rather than merit alone, which can also have a detrimental effect on IS development. Finally, management may simply be afraid of asking 'stupid' questions for fear of losing face (Collins and Bicknell 1997).

However, even without deliberate distortion on the part of participants in ISDs, there can be miscommunication and misunderstanding and a considerable degree of tension between different players in public sector ISDs. Professional groups have their own languages, their own ways of doing things, their own understanding of the world – what is generally called a 'culture'. Bureaucratic culture can sit uncomfortably with the individualistic, heroic culture of the programmer and the faddish culture of the management consultant and NPM-influenced managers (Figure 1.2). For example, while some writers on IT have alluded to the conservatism of IT engineers and their willingness to downplay what they can achieve (Glass 1999), most note the individualistic and heroic nature of the programming culture, where difficulties and possible failure are just further challenges to be solved by hugely talented programmers (Bronson 1999; Swanson 1988). This particular technological focus of many IT and IS specialists increases their inattentiveness to problems of failure and the appropriateness of the technology to the organisation – and, indeed, their resentment of and resistance to management, personal and political factors, and reporting requirements that might interfere with the technological puzzle at hand. As Lyytinen and Robey (1999: 94) note:

> The profession of ISD is characterized by specialized training and circumscribed theorizing. Since the dawn of business computing, training in IS has meant 'computer training', and IS professionals remain technologists at heart. Unfortunately, a technologist's perspective does not encourage an accurate diagnosis of the role of computing in business strategy and operations.

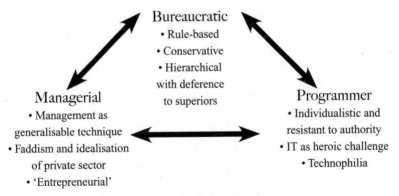

Figure 1.2. Culture Clashes in Information System Development

Indeed, the different professional values, modes of behaviour, language and belief systems of the different participants in ISDs can lead to some confusion and incommensurability, and a degree of 'talking past' each other. The risk-taking 'entrepreneurial' culture of managers and managerial consultants, and their often baffling jargon, may add to the confusion and the danger of failure, especially as NPM models and NPM-influenced managers and consultants often sit atop or beside largely traditional bureaucracies. Line management may find that giving orders to an individualistic, highly skilled and somewhat recalcitrant programmer does not have the desired effect. There can be considerable professional jealousies and 'turf protection', where attempts to direct other players are seen as unwarranted interference and as such are resisted in various ways – by restriction of information, for instance. Indeed, like any situation involving humans, ISDs involve political battles, struggles for individual autonomy, power and value dominance, career advancement, personality clashes, and so on (Knights and Murray 1994; Grover, Lederer, and Sabherwal 1988). The complexities of technological development are only further complicated by the complexities of human relations.

Even when problems are acknowledged, projects may continue because the forces encouraging abandonment are overpowered by the forces encouraging continuance – including those with a strong belief that 'it will be all right on the night'. In particular, what is called the completion effect – namely the nearness to the successful completion of the project – is a strong driving force. In IS development, this is especially relevant due to the '90 per cent completion' syndrome, where the proportion of the completed project increases readily to where it is estimated to be 90 per cent completed, but after that it increases very slowly (Abel-Hamid 1988). Some projects are reported to be 90 per cent complete for half their duration: an obvious impossibility. In a survey of IT auditors, it was found that the completion effect classified over 70 per cent of runaway projects (Keil, Mann, and Rai 2000).

Front-line staff can provide a 'reality check' on the overreaching ambitions of IS developers and management. However, critiques of bureaucratic structures have noted the tendencies of staff members to follow even misguided commands, and for responsibility and initiative to be discouraged (Merton 1957). In any event, 'front-line' grumbles may not be treated as carefully as they should, especially if the hierarchical culture sits (however uneasily) with public choice and new public management notions of management superiority and the treatment of professional groups as rent-seeking interest groups. Management hostility to even mild – and in retrospect, highly justified – reservations that front-line staff have expressed in IS developments has been noted in failures (see Chapters 3 and 4). On the other hand, a factor in failures can be the reluctance or inability of end users to adopt and adapt to the new technology, if the benefits of using the system are not seen as justifying the effort of relearning skills needed to use it, or where end-users actively subvert the computerisation process (Al-Gahtani and King 1999; Dinsdale 2004; Rocheleau 2003; Wilson and Howcroft 2002).

As such, developing systems without the involvement and, at very least, tacit approval of staff, can be a high-risk proposition.

Contracting Out

The popularity of new public management models has partly been in response to the perceived failings and rigidity of the bureaucratic model of government, as has the related growth of 'contracting-out'. Many, if not most, public sector ISDs are outsourced to private companies rather than developed in-house. Management and other consultancies are often hired to advise on IT and management system requirements, on purchasing arrangements, and to monitor and audit ISDs. However, there is considerable evidence that contracts are not effective in controlling projects and providing sanctions when IS projects fail, and that outsourcing has costs and dangers of its own. In the highly complex and changing environment of IS development, no contract, even if it runs for thousands of pages, can hope to foresee and control all aspects of an ISD (Collins and Bicknell 1997; Dale and Goldfinch 2002). The complex and uncertain causes of failure – if and when failure does occur – and the often remarkably complex contracts that have been developed in (a usually vain) attempt to control the development and provide sanctions, mean that in the face of failure, litigation can be costly and the results uncertain. Some IT companies have even been suspected of building penalty payments for late delivery of applications into their costings when tendering for contracts (see Chapter 6).

A number of studies similarly caution against an over-reliance on external consultants and information technology outsourcing. As Grant (2003: 173) notes:

> intended to save costs and develop competencies, I. T. outsourcing can be a double-edged sword if there is insufficient internal capacity for performing effective due diligence in I. T. systems procurement, designing and managing the outsourcing relationship and capturing and embedding new knowledge gained into the organisation.

Indeed, as Brown and Brudney (1998: 341) found, local governments with 'higher levels of contracting ... were less likely to have the project delivered on time and within budget and achieved less benefit from the technology in productivity and performance, organisation decision making, and customer service.' Very often, public sectors do not have the capacity, resources, and personnel to adequately develop and monitor outsourced projects, particularly as during the privatisation drives of the 1980s and 1990s government-owned computer and information technology agencies were often sold off. Higher levels of contracting can also impede the development of this capacity (Brown and Brudney 1998). In a number of countries, particularly developing ones, this lack of state capacity can be pronounced. This leaves potential for consultant and/or producer capture and for exploitative relationships, often between extremely large and powerful multinational IT and consultancy companies and comparatively less powerful and less competent governments: again, the risk of this is comparatively greater in developing countries with limited state capacity. Nor does competition provide a solution. In a marketplace there may be only a few large IT and consultancy companies. As such, contestability may not be sufficient to provide a check on potential capture by allowing competition during the tendering of contracts, and by allowing different companies to advise on purchasing as well as to develop, implement and maintain different parts of the system. In some cases, companies have absorbed rivals involved in developing different parts of a system during the process of ISD, further reducing competition and contestability and increasing the dangers of producer capture (Chapter 6). In any event, external consultants and suppliers are prone to the four enthusiasms outlined above. These issues are explored at greater length throughout this book.

The New Zealand Public Sector

In subsequent chapters we examine a number of information system developments, and failures in the New Zealand public sector, before examining public-sector information system monitoring regimes and drawing together lessons from our case studies. Chapter 2 opens by defining e-government and outlining e-government expectations. A series of e-government developmental phases are examined, from basic electronic provision of online information to genuine horizontal and vertical integration of government functions. E-government developments and strategy in Australia, Britain, and the United States and then in New Zealand are discussed and compared. Finally, the chapter outlines the intersection of e-government with other New Zealand public-sector developments, in particular the government's desire for greater attention to joint departmental policy outcomes. Again, expectations and rhetoric often outstrip results and we suggest (also drawing on our study of Landonline) that some e-government initiatives may not see the high usage anticipated. While many people are happy to search various government websites and electronic systems for information, they are more reluctant to engage in more sophisticated (and difficult to use) transactional activities. Furthermore, due to the general problems with ICT developments highlighted throughout this book, we posit that the e-government programme (including the eventual machinery of government 're-engineering') may well be overly ambitious, with many unanticipated consequences and costs.

Chapters 3 to 6 are in-depth case studies of e-government and ICT failures in the New Zealand public sector. Chapter 3 examines failures in the New Zealand health sector, particularly during the 1990s. Information collection was central to the government's market-oriented restructuring of the health sector during that era. However, successive governments and ministers paid minimal attention to ICT developments, leaving providers to develop their own systems. This led to multiple information systems, which undermined interoperability across the sector – a problem that remains to this day.

Chapter 4 details the purchase by Health Waikato, a public hospital cluster, of the Shared Medical Systems (SMS) information system. This was abandoned in mid-2000, only eighteen months after purchase, at a cost of $17 million. The SMS system was an inappropriate one, and Health Waikato did not undertake a rigorous needs assessment. With multiple and competing players – including a governing board as well as management and government representatives – decision-making was flawed and accountability for failure difficult to determine. The failure also highlighted that off-the-shelf systems designed for use in another country cannot be easily installed in a New Zealand organisation.

Chapter 5 examines the INCIS development in the New Zealand Police force, abandoned in 1999 after years of development at a direct cost of above $100 million, and with indirect costs largely incalculable. The INCIS fiasco was characterised by remarkably overblown expectations regarding ICT; the proposed use of highly sophisticated technology never successfully developed; personality conflicts; a naive reliance on a highly complex contract; changes in specifications in the project; continual budget and timetable overruns; reporting problems; and continual reassurances that the project would be completed. A number of management and reporting changes could not save the project.

Chapter 6 examines Landonline, a survey and title system operated by Land and Information New Zealand (LINZ). This was announced as finished in November 2003, although some work on the system continues. While deemed successful by LINZ, the project ran considerably over initial budget estimates, faced continual delays, and caused significant disruption to business during its development. This was despite a reasonably modest aim of automating existing processes, tightly controlled contracts, and a disposition to use existing technology. While its searching functions are widely applied, use of its more sophisticated transactional functions still remains below projections, considerably undermining expected financial benefits. The Landonline case provides useful cautions regarding e-government projects that might work in a technical sense but still face considerable user resistance and 'user failure'.

Our final chapter charts the evolution of ICT monitoring regimes in the New Zealand public sector from highly laissez-faire models, with agencies largely left to their own devices, to increasingly prescriptive regimes by the early 2000s. We draw together lessons from our case studies and the wider literature. While early failures such as INCIS were conceived under earlier monitoring regimes, later projects, such as Landonline and Health Waikato, also raise cautions regarding the new prescriptions. Some requirements are being ignored, and, even when followed, do not guarantee project success. We also argue that the New Zealand Government has not learnt one of the key lessons of continuing project failure: that large projects generally fail and should be avoided if possible. We conclude by restating our pessimism regarding ICT developments and caution against the enthusiasms of public sector information technology development and 'e-government'.

2.

What is 'E-government'?

Effective implementation of E-government is important in making Government more responsive and cost-effective (Bush 2002).

E-government uses improved Internet-based technology to make it easy for citizens and businesses to interact with the government, save taxpayer dollars, and streamline citizen-to-government communications (Bush 2002).

Ensuring that IT supports the business transformation of Government itself so that we can provide better, more efficient, public services (Blair 2005).

We see e-government enabling a transformation in the way government operates and delivers results for New Zealanders (Mallard 2003).

Like many trends that influence public policy and administration, 'e-government' is a multifaceted and nebulous idea, easily applied to a range of different situations across the entire gamut of government and society, and with differing intentions. Wide-ranging claims are made for e-government, considerable hopes are pinned on it, and substantial commitments – financial and otherwise – made to it. The concept has been embraced by political leaders and is being used to drive changes to the public sector, and to legitimise investment of public money in information technology (IT). Moreover, as governments progressively alter their e-government strategies (as noted in this chapter) in keeping with new policy initiatives and technology, the concept continues to evolve. For these reasons, it is important to explore the concept of 'e-government' in some detail. This chapter, therefore, considers these questions:

(1) What is 'e-government', what is expected of it, what is driving it and what are the implications for the structure and functions of the public sector?

(2) What are the developmental phases of e-government?

(3) What e-government strategies have governments developed, and what challenges have resulted from this?

(4) How does e-government New Zealand intersect with other public sector developments?

(1) What is E-government?

Broadly speaking, e-government might be defined as information and computer technology (ICT) and, specifically, internet and web-enabled public service activity: activity that computerisation facilitates or replaces. In keeping with this, any ICT activity within individual government departments or local authority offices might be described as e-government. More specifically, and following recent trends, e-government refers to the explicit coordination and oversight by central government of ICT activity, strategy and policy development, and of government and public services facilitated via the internet and related technologies. Central government does not necessarily feature within the broader definition. By contrast, in the more specific definition, central government plays a key role in terms of placing ICT at the centre of public sector work – indeed, of embracing ICT as a lever for the rejuvenation of the government and its relationships with the public – and providing direction for its development.

Governments around the world have adopted the notion of e-government for a range of reasons. These include the desire to lead the way in the development of the 'information economy' and keep up with increasing computerisation in the private sector, which in turn places pressure on government to match private sector developments. Related to this is the concept of 'competitive advantage'. In a globalised world, where capital flows freely between economies, governments place great importance on providing infrastructure that is attractive to foreign investors, including efficient public service systems and general 'wiredness', and presumably responsiveness, of the economy. Indeed, international business environment surveys routinely compare factors such as broadband penetration (see, for example, International Telecommunication Union 2005; Point Topic 2005).

Expectations of E-government

As noted, there are varying e-government expectations, both practical and theoretical. Broadly speaking, these may be branded 'managerial', 'government coordination and transformation', and 'participation.' These are discussed in the following sections.

Managerial

As Chadwick and May (2003) note, the *managerial* conceptualisation of e-government views ICT as a tool of efficient administration, responsive to the needs of the 'new [knowledge] economy', and faster delivery of services and information. Information flows are two-way (between government and consumers) and service centred, although the primary focus is on improving intra-government information exchange and capacity to deliver on predetermined government objectives. The logic of the system is 'service delivery', and policy and information presentation.

Following this, a key expectation – of politicians and government departments – is that e-government will produce more efficient communications and public service management by accelerating information flows, integrating information from disparate sources, and reducing public service staff numbers. Government departments traditionally collect information for their own use. ICTs give rise to information sharing via e-mail networks and inter-departmental websites. Moreover, the web facilitates the capacity for increased information gathering. In tandem, the need for paper communications is reduced, as is the need for a physical presence, as website information replaces front-counter officials. Around the globe, for example, government departments are progressively placing service information and official forms for services, such as business registrations and tax assessments, on their websites, to be downloaded and then resubmitted from any networked device.

A related expectation is that availability of government information and services will intensify; that government, in an environment increasingly concerned with transparency and contributing to development of the knowledge economy, will make documentation available on websites. Such material may include discussion documents, policy statements, and archival matter, and will be readily available to those with internet access. A collateral of this is the increasing prevalence of 'virtual' government, where policy implementation and public interactions take place via e-mail, websites and other ICT-enabled forums.

Government Coordination and Transformation

A second set of e-government expectations revolves around the notion of *government coordination and transformation* – that ICT will reverse 'fragmentation' across government, while centralising control of information and policy activity. Since the 1980s, public policy in the developed world has been concerned with devolving responsibilities to government agencies and developing incentives for them to pursue individual goals and outputs (Boston et al. 1996; Self 1993; Walsh 1995). Often termed 'managerialism', this has led to insular behaviour and problems with the coordination of government administration and policy (6 et al. 2002). The hope is that ICT will break down the barriers between the many agencies often involved in delivering services as they become interconnected. In so doing, the public sector and its services will become increasingly integrated and 'reconnected'. For the public, confusion over which agency to approach will be reduced. In keeping with this, the relevance of individual government departments will come under scrutiny, particularly where websites become the focus of, and point of interaction by, users of specific services. For example, in any developed country, every child, elderly person and welfare recipient would obtain services such as education, welfare, employment, social work and health from a range of agencies. Similarly, each agency involved in providing such services would collect relevant information on their clients and generate policy advice. Web 'portals' that integrate information about services for specific groups and provide links to disparate agencies promise to provide a 'one-stop' service and a focus for government agencies. In turn, government agencies would have incentives to work more closely with one another.

In line with the above, a further expectation is that public administration and policymaking will undergo a fundamental transformation from the traditional bureaucratic form, in which technocratically oriented officials are closely aligned with individual government departments, to the 'e-government paradigm' (Ho 2002). It is assumed that ICT facilitates and therefore shifts the emphasis towards building coordinated policy and service delivery networks. In an e-government world, work is routinely conducted beyond the physical boundaries of individual agencies. Networks of policymakers from across and beyond government, with relevant expertise around policy issues, are assembled and function in cyberspace. The result – in theory – is increased collaboration, improved policy capacity, and a heightened customer service focus, as well as reductions in the 'gap' between high-level central government policymakers and those implementing policy at the front-line of service delivery. The e-government paradigm, of course, challenges the institutional and physical foundations of government as the focus shifts towards information and services available via a single web-based contact point and away from individual government agencies. In accordance with this, governments need to examine how their agencies and policy work should be structured, funded, and monitored (Fountain 2001). For instance, should agencies remain independent administrative units, or should mergers and downsizings that align with web-based and electronic service delivery be pursued?

Participation

Drawing upon democratic theory, the notion of *participation* frames a third set of e-government expectations. There are two variations on this theme. The first is the idea of *consultation*, in which e-government is viewed as a tool for developing better policy responses to electronically articulated public needs. A core aim is to boost public education and involvement in policy and public service design. In contrast with the managerial model, the consultative model sees interest groups providing an important input into government policy (Chadwick and May 2003). In accordance with this, interest groups, agencies, associations and individuals may all interact and develop advocacy coalitions within 'cyberspace' and use information in the quest to influence government. E-government may also extend to the development of electronic democratic arrangements such as voting and referenda systems, opinion polling, and for feedback mechanisms such as advisory groups and electronic public meetings that augment the representative process.

The second participation variant stems from theories of '*deliberative*' or '*direct*' democracy (Norris 2003), capturing the ideals of free speech and rights of expression. From this perspective, e-government's aim is to enhance deliberation, participation and, ultimately, democracy. Unlike the consultative (and the managerial) model, where the state maintains a position of control, in the deliberative model the role of government is reduced to regulating infrastructure and mediating public exchange. Deliberation, in its purest form (or 'Habermasian' form after the social theorist Jurgen Habermas), conceives of political processes as governed by a shared aim of achieving a consensus, with no single interest or player exerting undue pressure or influence on proceedings. Information flows are complex and across an array of forums including discussion groups, e-mail list servers, interactive websites, mobile devices, and so forth. Researchers have found that the existence of the 'digital divide', between those who do and do not have e-mail and internet access, undermines the potential for deliberative democracy (Thomas and Streib 2005; Wicklund 2005). Universal computer access and the capacity to participate are, therefore, crucial to the deliberative democracy concept.

Fulfilling the Expectations

E-government clearly has elements that are relevant to both internal (within and across government and its agencies) and external (interactions between government and society) public sector functions, with widespread implications for the structure of the state. Of course, the expectations outlined above are simply expectations, and no country in the world is presently anywhere near fulfilling all of them. Furthermore, as noted, meeting these expectations hinges on the preferences and priorities of politicians and the public, as well as a variety of other factors for which the evidence is mixed. These include:

(1) that ICTs and the information made available via them are user-friendly;

(2) that the information that agencies might encounter in their data-gathering is readily accessible and digestible;

(3) that the public and businesses have access to computers and prefer to interact with government services in this way.

Research in the United States shows that its citizens actively use e-mail and the internet for 'informational' services such as recreation and tourism. However, 'transactional' e-government services are much less used; for example, only 15 per cent of tax forms are submitted online (Reddick 2005; Thomas and Streib 2003). In addition, visitors to government websites are more likely to be university educated and well-off, confirming a digital divide between those who do and do not engage with e-government (Thomas and Streib 2005).

The fulfilment of promises such as reduced fragmentation rely not only on robust ICT development and availability of technologies that will assist inter-agency collaboration. Good working relationships between groups and agencies involved in service delivery are also required, as well as the identification of issues and services conducive to inter-agency delivery. Without tight inter-agency coordination, service users, expecting the seamless service they were promised, may find that, if difficulties arise, they still have to deal with individual agencies. Similarly, there is no example yet in the world of ICTs driving a genuinely integrated government whose separate agencies are not identifiable. Whether transparency will increase is also questionable: it may be that only information deemed relevant or tailored for public consumption will be placed on websites; that much of the internal e-mail communication and work that feeds into policy will not be placed in agency archives, thereby defying scrutiny; and that the increased volume of available information will actually confuse the public.

Naturally, in keeping with ICT advances, procurement and application, and the development of public policy, e-government is an evolutionary process. Some parts of government will be more digitised than others, and some expectations will be easier to achieve than others. The factors affecting this include strategic commitment to ICT procurement strategies and website development, financial and human resources and, of course, the nature of the activity (some departments, such as immigration and tax collection, will have more public interaction than others, such as finance and statistics, which work at a higher data generation and policy advisory level). E-government development also relies on the commitment of government and its agencies, the extent to which the 'e' means simply computerising existing government functions as opposed to transforming the organisation, as well as public trust and satisfaction with electronic systems. Finally, political leaders may promote some dimensions of e-government more than others. Researchers in Austria found that politicians there readily promoted 'e-government' for improving administration, but showed minimal interest in developing 'e-democracy' because this would reduce their power and control (Mahrer and Krimmer 2005).

(2) Developmental Phases of E-government

Various writers (e.g. Layne and Lee 2001; Norris 2001; Silcock 2001; Torres, Pina, and Acerete 2005) have discussed the 'phases' of e-government development, providing a framework for understanding the advancement of ICT application. In the first phase, attention is on the electronic cataloguing of information to be presented in online form. This phase involves government departments creating websites containing basic information about their services, downloadable forms and documents, and contact details. Communication in this model is essentially 'one way': from government to client.

The second phase, moving toward 'two-way' communication, involves the development of more sophisticated websites that link internal government systems with an online presence, allowing citizens to interact with government electronically.

For example, many transactions – such as paying of fines, registering for services and completing tax returns – can then be conducted electronically. In this phase, close attention must be paid to security issues and technical detail. Systems for online transactions, for instance, need to be designed to ensure that the public can have confidence in them. Furthermore, data obtained from the public should be automatically transferred to the correct internal systems, as opposed to manually redirected or re-entered by data entry personnel.

In the third phase, which might be termed 'vertical integration', individual local agencies and their services become connected with central systems. This phase has particular relevance in countries with federal systems of government, such as Australia and the United States, where state and central government agencies are often disconnected, despite the fact that each 'level' of government is responsible for implementing federal government policy. In countries such as New Zealand, this phase would see local government and the many regional agencies that are contracted to provide government services being linked together so that any interaction with a local service would be automatically relayed to relevant central agencies. This third phase sees the development of 'portal' websites that bring together in a structured fashion a range of services in one website that is the vehicle for a number of agencies, both central and local, largely developed around function. Thus, portals facilitate the 'clustering' and integration of common services. Examples include portals for financial and business services (in both government and the private sector), welfare and health services, and customs and immigration services. Members of the public would also be able to build their own customised portals that link the desired services of different agencies.

The fourth phase sees genuine 'horizontal integration' of government services. Clients will not experience any 'walls' between services and agencies, as systems will have become fully integrated, interactive and interoperable. Instead of the public having to navigate their way around agencies (or portals) to obtain or transact with various services, transactions take on an apparently seamless quality. Clients would have 'one-stop' access to government services. This, of course, may have implications for the structure of government, as Silcock (2001: 90) suggests: 'in some cases, new departments will have formed from the remains of predecessors. Others will have the same names, but their interiors will look nothing like they did before e-Government'.

Most of the world's governments have reached at least the first phase. Many have moved into the second phase. The first three phases can be seen as 'add ons' to existing public sector structures and work processes, and do not in themselves demand institutional adaptation. The third and fourth phases require much more sophisticated ICT, while the fourth, in particular, necessitates substantial redesign of public sector work, organisational re-engineering and government restructuring. The hurdles to the achievement of vertical and horizontal integration are, therefore, much greater than the simple e-mail and web-presence required of the first two phases. Implicit in phases three and four is also an assumption that the technology and technical personnel implementing these are available, capable, and reliable and able to fulfil the promises of e-government. The case studies discussed in the following chapters of this book illustrate, however, that a myriad of problems – some stemming from budgetary or institutional issues, others the consequence of inadequate project monitoring, over-confidence in the capabilities of ICT systems, and the complexity of service provision and organisation – are likely to pose significant challenges on the way to phases three and four. The lesson here is that policymakers should exercise caution in the planning, advocacy for and adoption of new technologies.

(3) International E-government Developments

'E-government' is the latest in a long line of trends in public administration that have swept the globe and influenced the focus and shape of government and public policy. Most nations have implemented elements of e-government to varying degrees (Norris 2001). Many governments have embarked upon wide-ranging and ambitious advancement programmes. This section reviews developments in Australia, Britain, the United States, and New Zealand.

Australia

Australia was relatively early and swift to embrace the e-government concept. In 1997, as part of his *Investing for Growth* policy statement, Prime Minister John Howard highlighted the importance of ICT as a driver of national prosperity. In line with this, he announced a series of initiatives including: first, that all Commonwealth government agencies aim to have appropriate services available on-line by December 2001; second, a Government Information Centre be established through the Office for Government Online as a main access point for information about government services; third, electronic payments become the normal means for the Commonwealth by 2000; and, fourth, a government-wide intranet be created for communication between government departments. This was followed up, in 1998, by *Strategic Framework for the Information Economy*, which outlined ten priority areas for the information economy including skills, infrastructure, e-commerce, industry development, health, culture and regulation, as well as additional detail of the government's approach to providing online services (National Office for the Information Economy 1998).

In 2000, in response to the rapidly growing numbers of Australians using the internet, the Commonwealth government unveiled its *Government Online* strategy (National Office for the Information Economy 2000). This was aimed at readying government for the expected demand for online services, but also at ensuring a common framework for government online service development. Essentially, the strategy was to allow government departments to plan and deliver their own online presence against a backdrop of cross-governmental coordination and governance by the Office of Government Online. This cross-governmental approach is commonplace, in keeping with the e-government aim of ensuring interoperability, and has also been adopted in New Zealand as discussed below. *Government Online* outlined eight high-level 'strategic priorities', but also listed 'specific actions' required of government agencies. For example, Priority 1 required agencies to 'take full advantage of opportunities provided by the internet', stipulated that each agency should develop an Online Action Plan derived from an audit of all services; an analysis of e-services that might be delivered in collaboration with other agencies; a timeframe for placing functions online; and an inventory of impediments to be overcome to achieve the Prime Minister's 2001 target for online services. *Government Online* also provided information on data standards and information exchange protocols that agencies were expected to comply with, as well as outlining an expectation that agencies would identify stakeholders and consult with them.

Since *Government Online*, the pace of 'strategic policy' and e-government service development has increased. An updated strategy issued in 2002 (National Office for the Information Economy 2002) reinforced the desire for secure and trustworthy cross-government service integration. Meanwhile, the Office of Government Online was renamed the National Office for the Information Economy and then, in 2004, the Australian Government Information Management Office (Agimo – see www.agimo.gov.au). Later in 2004, Agimo was made a business unit of the Commonwealth Department of Finance and Administration. Agimo continues to produce policy documents on e-government issues such as security, information infrastructure, and national guidelines for developments within Australia's seven state-level governments. Notably, each state government has its own e-government office, leading to several state differences. This is complicating the administration of e-government development and countering interoperability goals. Moreover, a recent Audit Office report noted that, due to the lack of evaluation built into e-government development, key agencies were failing to measure the effectiveness of their advances in ICT and thus were unable to determine whether services had improved or whether the government was getting good value for money (Australian National Audit Office 2005).

While international studies have consistently ranked Australia among the world leaders in terms of e-government and internet usage (e.g. United Nations Public Administration Network 2004), it is fair to suggest that Australian developments are still in their infancy. While most Australian Commonwealth and state government departments have achieved the first two developmental phases outlined above, movement into the next two stages – vertical and horizontal integration – remains largely in the planning and piloting phases. This reflects the difficulties and magnitude (and perhaps even the impossibility) of re-engineering the policy and practical initiatives of multiple organisations to ensure integration. Recognising this, in 2004 Agimo commissioned the Institute of Public Administration Australia to produce a series of papers on the challenges ahead. These noted the promise of e-government, but also the considerable number of issues to be surmounted if e-government aims are to be achieved (Halligan and Moore 2004). A particular issue, given the isolation and disadvantages that many Australian communities face, is how to realise the promise of creating access for all to online services (Dugdale et al. 2005).

Britain

E-government came to the centre of the British government agenda in 1996 with the release by the Conservative government of *Government.Direct* (Central Information Technology Unit 1996). Through harnessing ICT, this aimed for better and more efficient government services, improved transparency and cost savings. *Government. Direct* failed to attract much political attention, but presaged developments propelled by the subsequent New Labour government. The vision and strategy for e-government were outlined in a series of papers (Cabinet Office 1998; Cabinet Office 1999) that form part of New Labour's 'modernisation' programme. This has objectives to centralise and better coordinate policymaking, build more responsive and collaborative government, and engage with the public. Key elements of the e-government initiative included a commitment to make 25 per cent of government services available online by 2002 and 100 per cent by 2008.

In 2000, a more detailed e-government plan was released (Cabinet Office 2000). This extended the deadline for all government services to be electronically available to 2005. Reflecting the scope of e-government and range of issues to be worked through, literally dozens of papers and press releases have been issued since then. These include policy papers and policy announcements, in an attempt to increase use of technology in government; collaboration with private agencies; and movement from paper to electronically based information and communication systems. In addition, a succession of new institutional arrangements has been introduced. These include creation of an e-minister, an Office of the e-Envoy (replaced in 2004 by the Office of E-Government), and individual departmental 'information age government champions' charged with advancing change at the agency level. Such initiatives have launched an industry of further policy papers, goal-setting, progress reports and press releases. Furthermore, e-government development has required considerable coordination across a range of implicated government policy units, agencies and other institutions such as the central Performance Innovation Unit, Central Information Technology Unit, Policy Action Team, Parliament, industry and non-government groups.

By late 2004, 75 per cent of services (largely informational and some transaction services) identified as capable of being e-enabled had been made available online, with the prediction that the target set in 2000 would be 96 per cent achieved by the end of 2005 (Cabinet Office 2004). However, the head of the E-Government Office suggested this was only a start; that key future priorities should include: developing a national identification framework; ensuring that every government agency has a Chief Information Officer; making sure that online services are accessible and used by all people (three-quarters of UK citizens had never visited a government website); and that web-enabled services alter the way people interact with government (European E-Government Observatory 2004).

There is much hinging on future British e-government developments as, in 2004, the government directly linked e-government investment to reductions, by 2008, of over 84,000 people in the civil service. This is predicted to result from reducing administrative costs and 'back-office' functions (Brown 2004). In addition, in mid-2005, the government announced its intention to establish an 'IT Academy' aimed at nurturing public sector ICT experts (European E-Government Observatory 2004).

In tandem with e-government, the New Labour government has also put considerable effort into developing 'joined-up government' (JUG), another strand of the modernisation programme. JUG corresponds with and is in part driven by e-government developments. JUG essentially refers to the achievement of horizontally and vertically integrated public sector activity. It seeks to alleviate contradictions between different government policies and agency work, reduce duplication, increase the flow of ideas and cooperation across government, and create 'seamless' public services (6 et al. 2002; Pollitt 2003).

The assumptions about e-government discussed earlier in this chapter underpin developments in Britain. Namely, that ICT will sharpen efficiency, modernise government and make it more accessible, and increase citizen involvement. Various observers have noted the strong managerial focus implicit in British e-government developments (e.g. Chadwick and May 2003; Holliday 2001; Hudson 2002).

The United States

With the 1993 launch of the National Performance Review (NPR), the United States was an early convert to the notion of ICT-driven government. Coordinated out of the then Vice President Al Gore's office, the NPR viewed ICT as an essential factor in the 'reinvention' of government, and that through its application the relationship between government and citizens would be 're-engineered'. The NPR focus was unashamedly managerial. An initial expectation was that ICT would result in significant savings as paperwork, administrative and staffing costs were reduced through computerisation. By 1998, when the NPR was renamed the National Partnership for Reinventing Government, it was claimed that ICT application had reduced the federal workforce by 351,000 people and saved US$137 billion in public spending (Fountain 2001: 21).

From 1998, e-government work was more service oriented and focused on developing 'virtual agencies', which bring together disparate services, and inter-agency e-government initiatives. There are similarities here with British developments. By 2000, a wide range of virtual agencies (with services ranging from those relevant to elderly and children, to those for business, state services, and education) had established a web presence via the federal FirstGov portal (Chadwick and May 2003). Considerable effort has gone into creating virtual agencies and networks. For example, the International Trade Data System integrates and facilitates the work of around sixty-three agencies with involvement in trade; the 'US Business Advisor' portal, through which small business online loans can be approved, regulations checked and opportunities listed, is an interactive interorganisational network for six federal agencies (Fountain 2001).

Developments have intensified since 2002, when President George W. Bush unveiled his 'Presidential E-Government Strategy', which resulted in the *E-Government Act 2002*. This outlined the aims of ICT as a driver of inter-agency collaboration and 'results-oriented' citizen engagement, various standards for e-government, as well as initiatives such as allowing private ICT providers to take a share in savings achieved through services provided to government agencies. E-government development across the United States is presently presided over by the Office of Electronic Government and Information Technology, based in the federal Office of Management and Budget. This office oversees the government's approximately US$60 billion invested annually in ICT.

Progress since the 2002 Act was highlighted in a 2004 report. This noted that only half the federal government agencies were managing ICT in accordance with the 2002 standards and had no ICT skills gaps, that only 75 per cent had established acceptable business cases for all their systems, and that 90 per cent had properly secured systems. The report also highlighted the growing numbers of people using online services to pay taxes, establish businesses, and so forth (Office of Management and Budget 2004). In the March 2005 scorecard on progress in implementing the President's Management Agenda, only nine out of twenty-six executive agencies achieved a 'green' result – which indicates success, as measured by the President's Office, in e-government implementation (see http://www.whitehouse.gov/results/agenda/scorecard.html). Despite this, the United States was ranked number one in the 2004 United Nations e-government readiness index (United Nations Public Administration Network 2004).

Of course, the individual North American states, each with their own government, also have e-government offices and strategies, further complicating interoperability and consistent country-wide development. Compared with Britain, with its government-controlled and funded National Health Service, areas such as health care pose particular problems for United States e-government. Considerable effort is required to bring together the numerous insurers, payers and service providers – both public and private. So far, portals have provided only information that assists health system navigation. In 2005, recognising the potential gains of ICT-enabled health care, a bi-partisan group of senators, backed by calls from the president, announced their intention to introduce legislation to create a nationwide electronic health records system (Commonwealth Fund 2005).

The increasing incidence of computer hacking, spam e-mail, and viruses, which pose substantial costs to industry (and private computer users) in terms of lost productivity and damage, is inciting calls within the United States for government oversight of the internet. To date, government has relied on the voluntary efforts of industry to produce virus-resistant software and more secure systems; by contrast, automobile industry standards are subject to stringent government regulation. There are widespread views about what sort of central controls are needed, and which agency (e.g. the new Department of Homeland Security) should provide oversight, which the government is carefully considering. The government itself is a major internet user and has concerns about the use of the internet by terrorist groups. It is highly likely, therefore, that the United States federal government will eventually move into some form of regulatory role (*New York Times* 1 September 2003).

New Zealand

Since 2000, when an E-Government Unit was established within the State Services Commission, there has been strong political commitment to e-government in New Zealand. Underpinning this has been the approach of the Labour-led government, elected in 1999, whose policies share characteristics with Britain's New Labour government. In contrast to the market approaches of the fourth Labour government (1984–90) and the National government (1990–9, with National-led coalition from 1996–9), the Labour coalition government has pursued a broadly social democratic agenda. Its rhetoric has focused on boosting public participation and collaboration in public affairs, building social cohesion and an inclusive economy, reducing inequalities, and enhancing the business environment. As a result, the government has implemented policies that devolve decision-making and resources to agencies and local communities, together with strong central direction via prescriptive policy strategies and accountability structures. It has also sought greater cross-governmental coordination and 'joined-up' government. E-government is seen as a means of achieving such goals.

Somewhat behind its Australian, British and American counterparts, New Zealand's first e-government strategy was released in April 2001. A year earlier the government announced its e-government 'vision', which stated that: 'New Zealanders will be able to gain access to government information and services and participate in democracy using the internet and ICTs as they emerge'.

New Zealand e-government policy and developments have thus been firmly within the 'managerial' paradigm. Although there appears to have been genuine interest in engaging the public, this has extended to no more than the provision of interactive e-services. Since 2005, something of a policy shift has been evident, with more explicit recognition of the capacity for ICT to build communities and public interaction (see, for example, Ministry of Economic Development 2005), although commitment to this has so far been largely rhetorical.

The April 2001 strategy outlined a variety of aims (Mallard 2001a). Principal aims were that New Zealand would be a world leader in e-government and that, by 2004, the internet would be the dominant means by which the public (and government itself) accessed government services and information. Behind these aims were a series of specific e-government objectives including: better and more convenient service via a 'one-stop shop' portal; more cost-effective and efficient government; leadership through supporting development of a knowledge economy through public sector innovation; an improved reputation for New Zealand as an information age economy; and greater public participation in government. In terms of public sector structure, the strategy envisaged both a 'seamless' service access and a 'seamless back office' (or reduced fragmentation among government departments) built through a common technology infrastructure.

The 2001 strategy listed a series of policy development and infrastructure milestones for completion by June 2002. These involved establishing a Secure Electronic Environment (SEE) to enable safe information exchange; a 'metadata' framework to ensure standard information cataloguing to make public access straightforward; a web portal strategy and standards; a framework (later called 'e-GIF' – e-government interoperability framework) for common data policies and standards to ensure that government services can be connected; and a National Information Infrastructure Protection Strategy (NIIPS) to protect against hacking. The achievement of these goals was seen as the collective responsibility of government agencies. The E-Government Unit of the State Services Commission was charged with setting the strategy in motion, assisting with and coordinating the work of agencies, and monitoring progress.

In December 2001, the strategy was updated (Mallard 2001b). The 'update' earmarked higher-level issues needing attention – such as governance, funding and the measuring of e-government effectiveness – largely to reflect political thinking about the longer-term implications of e-government. A 2003 update confirmed previous policy directions and was primarily an exercise in promoting the government's approach to the public and implicated agencies: essentially that central frameworks, protocols and goals had been established and should be adhered to. For instance, the 2003 update overviewed the government's 'service delivery architecture', which 'shows how the Government expects agencies to use and be a part of the government information, technology, and standards environment in the future' (Mallard 2003: 16). The update also noted that the e-government strategy applied not just to central but also local government. Of particular significance, the update timetabled two important milestones, stating that:

- by 2007, ICT will be integral to delivery of government services, and
- by 2010, the operation of government will have been transformed by the internet.

Achievements listed in the 2003 update included development of basic standards for e-government and, at a practical level, an increasing range of online services accessible via the government portal (www.govt.nz). The portal incorporates the services of around ninety government agencies and eighty-six local authorities. Again, security and, by implication, trust in e-government, governance, funding, and data quality standards and management topped the 'growing' list of 'challenges ahead' (Mallard 2003: 23). Governance (the management and guiding of ICT and e-government developments) poses particular challenges as agencies become interconnected. The strategy noted three facets of this: governance of shared inputs (joint use of information and technology), outputs (integrated service delivery), and between levels of government (central and local). In the government's view, governance requires developing methodologies for 'allocating decision-rights over shared inputs' and accounting for contributions to outputs. Funding also poses problems as 'it is hard to separate e-government funding from normal departmental expenditure on information and communication technologies' and 'the quantum of e-government funding required in future is currently unknown' (Mallard 2003: 24).

A 2004 e-government progress report produced various findings. It noted that the internet had become a dominant means of accessing government services – particularly for those working in government – but that only around 28 per cent of the public regularly used the internet for engaging with government. Sixty-seven per cent of agency websites were found to be of a high or good standard, while the quality of 'metadata' (high-level data for cataloguing information) was generally high. In terms of reducing fragmentation in government, the report found that most online services remained rooted in individual agencies, requiring users to contact several agencies in order to complete government transactions. Finally, the report noted that, while there appeared to be public demand for e-government, there was a lack of public knowledge about the information and services that government agencies supply online (State Services Commission 2004).

In mid-2005, the government launched a new draft *Digital Strategy* document. Led by the Ministry of Economic Development, this aimed at pushing forward an agenda to use ICT to bring together government, business, and communities 'for the benefit of all New Zealanders'. Outlined in the *Strategy* are a range of initiatives, from increasing broadband uptake (New Zealand has a high-level of internet use but is at the bottom of the OECD countries in terms of broadband penetration), to improving business and government productivity (Ministry of Economic Development 2005). Also in mid-2005, the State Services Commission was relaunched with a new and broader government leadership and development role. The E-Government Unit, housed in the State Services Commission and responsible for coordinating e-government developments, was subsumed within a new Information and Communication Technologies Branch. The 2007 and 2010 goals listed above were linked as one of the six new development goals for the State Services Commission, namely to 'use technology to transform the provision of services for New Zealanders' (State Services Commission 2005).

(4) E-government and Other State Sector Developments in New Zealand

How e-government fits with other state sector developments is an important question, particularly as, in tandem with e-government, the government is presiding over major changes to the focus and organisation of central government. These changes stem from the 2001 *Review of the Centre* (ROC) report (Mallard and Cullen 2001) commissioned and endorsed by Cabinet. The ROC grew out of concern at the proliferation of central agencies in the 1990s, and the apparently fragmented and uncoordinated nature of public services, and policy advice resulting from this, as well as the split between policy and operations agencies.

The 'major finding' of the ROC was that 'significant shifts in emphasis [of the public management system] are needed to better respond to the needs of the future' (Mallard and Cullen 2001: 4). The ROC made two key recommendations relevant to e-government. The first was the need to integrate service delivery around issues, such as children's services, where multiple agencies (health, education, welfare, and child and family services) are involved. The second was the need to reduce fragmentation. This entailed improving the 'alignment' between agencies through 'establishing networks of related agencies'. Extending this concept, the ROC recommended 'an accountability and reporting system that puts more emphasis on outcomes and high level priorities, as well as output specification' and 'gradual structural consolidation [including the] possibility of going much further, to formally group and manage Government agencies in 7–10 super networks' (Mallard and Cullen 2001: 5).

Although only a brief appendix was dedicated to the subject, the ROC noted that the e-government initiative was particularly relevant to implementing its recommendations. For example, the standardisation of information systems was seen as a facilitator of cross-agency information sharing, and the 'service' focus of e-government would reinforce the desired emphasis on outcomes that agencies deliver rather than the organisational structures doing the delivering (Mallard and Cullen 2001: 64).

Since the ROC report there have been a number of developments germane to e-government. For instance, under the 'Managing for Outcomes' programme, all thirty-six core government agencies have been required to deliver annual Statements of Intent that detail the desired 'priority' outcomes (where the agency wants to go, and what it wants to achieve) and the outputs (what the agency is doing, and how it is 'managing for outcomes') that show the agency is working towards its outcomes (Steering Group Managing for Outcomes 2002). Significantly, the new focus has required agencies to work closely with one another to identify common outcomes and outputs that impact on one another's work. For example, in order to work towards its desired outcome of 'People with high-quality working lives in thriving and inclusive communities', the Department of Labour must work with counterparts such as Treasury, Social Development, Health, Education and Housing. Agencies must ensure that their desired outcomes are appropriate and complement those of other agencies. They must also identify how they plan to work together. In the light of this, amendments to the Public Finance Act, which came into force in early 2005, allow for ministers and departments to share responsibility for joint budgets. Such activity, of course, is seen as being buttressed by initiatives stemming from the e-government strategy.

Finally, shifts in the role and focus of the State Services Commission indicate that e-government objectives are no longer a government 'add on', but have become central to state sector development. As noted earlier in this chapter, from mid-2005, the State Services Commission's revised aim has been to facilitate six new development goals that provide direction for the entire public sector. One of these goals is to ensure that e-government transforms New Zealand's public services.

Conclusion

'E-government' promises radical shifts in the way the public sector is organised and conducts its work, and in how the public navigates and accesses services. E-government is presently in an embryonic state, both in overseas countries and in New Zealand. Numerous expectations and strategies are espoused by political and technology leaders, multiple initiatives are in progress, and considerable gains are anticipated. Furthermore, it is clear that there is an element of 'sloganeering' attached to 'e-government' as a useful rhetorical device meaning all things to all people. It can be a managerial tool for creating efficiencies and cost-cutting; a lever for better coordination of policy, administration and the organisation of government; and a vessel for enhanced participation, deliberation, and democracy.

There are numerous unknowns, however, about the practice of e-government. It remains unclear, for instance, whether its promises will transpire or, as noted above, ICT will simply be an 'add on' to existing institutional arrangements with substantial additional costs. The issues surrounding implementation of e-government strategies and projects are complex and depend on many overlaying and interconnected factors – social, organisational, legal and, of course, technical, as well as resources and expectations. Moreover, e-government is a mammoth project in its own right for the simple fact that it applies to the entire public sector. When considered in the light of the fact that the great majority of public sector ICT projects fail in one way or another, there may be cause for pessimism about whether the much broader e-government project can be achieved or, if it is, whether its shape, functioning, and costs match predictions. Recent New Zealand experience with public-sector ICT projects, discussed in the subsequent chapters of this book, demonstrates that problems with governance, project implementation, and cost overruns are endemic. The cause of such problems may be attributed to:

- the overzealousness of ICT consultants and public officials responsible for implementing ICT policy;
- the application of technologies designed for purposes other than public work or the specific project they have been procured for;
- drastic miscalculations of the costs of ICT projects and challenges to their completion;
- mistaken beliefs about user acceptability;
- inadequate project monitoring.

Thus, there are grounds for scepticism about the benefits e-government will deliver.

3.

ICT in New Zealand's Health Sector:
A story of lost opportunity

Health care ICT in most advanced nations faces several challenges. These stem from the fact that government only partially funds the health system, and health services are delivered by a multitude of public and private providers based in community and institutional settings. Moreover, patients are likely to visit a number of providers in their health system encounters. In tandem, government is reliant on the health system for data, while information sharing between providers is today viewed as crucial to effective health care delivery.

In the publicly funded component of the health sector (in New Zealand, 80 per cent of all health expenditure is public, and public hospitals are dominant), there is the additional challenge of political leadership and facilitation of ICT policy and development. In New Zealand, this also impacts on the broader health sector, as much publicly funded health care is carried out by non-government providers, as it is for primary care. Thus, when, as happened through the decade of the 1990s, politicians completely restructured the health care system three times, the shock waves are felt far and wide. Against the backdrop of that restructuring, this chapter looks at information management and ICT development in the New Zealand health sector through the 1990s and into the new millennium. The story is one of lost opportunities, political negligence, shifting ideas about health policy and the shape of the health system, and the development of a Byzantine ICT topography.

Broadly speaking, the chapter probes two questions. First, did New Zealand's political leaders (effectively, the ultimate managers of the health sector) provide sufficient policy framework and leadership for ICT development through the 1990s? The short answer is 'no'. Second, have political leaders learnt the importance of robust ICT policy and institutional arrangements and that they have a pivotal role in achieving this? The response is a qualified 'probably'.

In general, the health system restructuring of the 1990s was damaging for information management and the development of ICT. Problems identified at the start of the decade remained unresolved some ten years later. These problems included poor data quality, lack of standards, difficulties with information exchange, poor coordination of data collections and systems, and inadequate information system governance. At least three information strategies were issued during the 1990s. Each time a new strategy was developed, and its implementation started to move forward, it was derailed by restructuring and a corresponding policy and organisational vacuum. Meanwhile, in the absence of central policy or oversight, agencies and networks within the sector continued to develop data collections and deploy ICT in isolation from one another. On the downside, this sowed the seeds of a myriad of problems stemming from the fact that the foundations of New Zealand's contemporary health information systems were laid in an era when competition, secrecy, and sector-driven developments were considered appropriate principles for health system design and organisation. In the latter part of the decade, there was a policy shift toward intersectoral collaboration and information sharing, requiring interoperability. The fundamentals for this were simply not available, and this is still true today. On a more positive note, the hands-off approach of the 1990s led to the development of a variety of localised examples of ICT systems, including at least one, in the Counties Manukau District Health Board, that is now at the forefront of international developments. With appropriate sector leadership, such examples could have been repeated across the entire health sector.

Since 2001, when the fourth consecutive strategy, the WAVE (Working to Add Value through E-information) report (WAVE Advisory Board 2001) was produced, there has been evidence of growing inter-provider and inter-regional collaboration, bringing with it increasing information sharing and interoperability projects. Both planners and the providers themselves have been driving this, as has government policy. While government policy presently places high importance on information management and ICT, this is countered by the fact that there is no single central institution responsible for information governance. Thus, the lack of ICT planning and coordination through the 1990s has given way to an environment in which central government agencies and units are one of many players in health care ICT, doing their best to provide gentle direction and support for incremental sector-driven developments.

In August 2005, a fifth information strategy, building on the WAVE recommendations, was launched (Health Information Strategy Steering Committee 2005). Recognising the embeddedness and complexity of ICT arrangements, this committee largely reflects and formalises developments occurring in the health sector. It also provides a plan for improving interoperability and information sharing, and expanding the reach of ICT connectivity within a national framework. The 2005 strategy highlights the fact that, because of preceding developments and health system structure, government is not in a position to take the lead and that New Zealand's highly devolved health system means 'each organisation … needs to take responsibility for their own strategic information system plans to guide development of solutions to their unique business challenges' (Health Information Strategy Steering Committee 2005: 17).

Health System Restructuring in New Zealand

Throughout the 1990s, when information management and technology came to prominence in health policy agendas, and when the government had a genuine opportunity to design and implement a comprehensive, long-term strategy for health information, New Zealand had four consecutive health care structures. In-depth details of the structures, change processes, and their impacts are available elsewhere (Cumming and Mays 2002; Gauld 2001; Gauld 2003). This section simply provides a brief overview. The first of the structures, the area health board (AHB) system, replaced an antiquated configuration of over thirty local hospital boards. The AHB system consisted of fourteen decentralised, geographically–based AHBs, financed by government and responsible for planning and funding an integrated range of services based on the assessed needs of their respective populations. Gradual implementation commenced in the mid-1980s, and the system was fully functional by 1989. The health sector was reviewed twice in the late 1980s (Gibbs, Fraser, and Scott 1988; Scott, Fougere, and Marwick 1986). Both reviews noted that information management was poor, with data incomplete, laden with inconsistencies and unreliable. There was no clarity, for instance, over how many patients were being treated and where, how much services were costing, or how efficient services were.

The National government elected in 1990 chose to restructure the health system to fit with its political preferences, and unveiled a 'competitive market system' for implementation by mid-1993. AHB functions were to be split, with needs assessment and purchasing responsibilities going to four new regional health authorities (RHAs) and provision to twenty-three hospital-based crown health enterprises (CHEs). CHEs were required to 'compete' with one another and any other private or non-government providers for service contracts offered for tender by the RHAs. In this period of 'market' ideals, there was little concern for national planning or coordination of the health care system: purchasers and providers developed their own arrangements to deliver on the government's goals for health care. Crucial to the competitive system was information to inform the service contracting process (approximately 8000 contracts were managed by the four RHAs). Purchasers and providers all required a reliable knowledge of how many services were in existence, how many patients were receiving them, and how much they cost. The competitive system was burdened with administrative and other problems, and another restructuring was announced following the 1996 general election.

The next system saw the four RHAs combined into one nationalised Health Funding Authority (HFA), while the CHEs were renamed hospital and health services. The system was to focus on public service, national consistency, and patient equity. No sooner had the HFA system been pulled into place, a process which took the best part of two years, than the 1999 election produced a change of government (Labour-led coalition) and another restructuring commenced. Again, fundamental change was required to create a system that resembled the earlier AHB system. The HFA was dissolved, with its functions split between the Ministry of Health and twenty-one semi-elected district health boards (DHBs). Within the funding allocated by the Ministry of Health, DHBs are responsible for needs assessments, planning, prioritising, and purchasing integrated services for their populations.

Despite the incessant restructuring many initiatives and institutions have persisted. These include Pharmac, an agency established in 1992 by the RHAs to manage the pharmaceutical schedule; services operated by and for indigenous Maori; the use of service funding and accountability contracts; and independent practitioner associations, which are groups of publicly subsidised general practitioners who clustered together for enhanced negotiating power with the RHAs. Since 2001, propelled by government policy (King 2001a), Primary Health Organisations have also entered the primary care landscape.

Information Policy and ICT through the Four Systems

As noted, reviews in the 1980s highlighted the key role of information systems. During the 1990s, information was brought to centre stage. However, as this section outlines, progress was variable despite a succession of high-level information management strategies, and problems that were identified at the start of the decade remained unresolved at its end. The section begins with the following overview of the strategies and related developments.

1991: The First Ministerial Strategy

In 1991, the first ministerial strategy for health information was issued, largely in response to an identified need for robust information in the pending competitive environment, but also to push findings of earlier review work onto the policy agenda. For instance, a 1990 report on the role and activities of the National Health Statistics Centre had recommended the need for a 'comprehensive and strategic national health information system for New Zealand' (Jack *et al.* 1990). A joint venture between the Department of Health and AHBs, the ensuing 1991 strategy noted that:

> Over the past two decades a number of initiatives originating within area health boards and from the Departments of Health and Statistics have attempted to improve the value of health information available throughout the health sector. These have had little success due to a lack of coordination and a lack of adequate funding. Until recently such initiatives were not part of an overall policy plan or strategy for the health sector (Williamson 1991: 1).

The 1991 strategy resulted from a considerable amount of work. Fourteen working groups were convened, eight to review various aspects of health information collection and management, the remaining six to review datasets maintained by the Health Statistical Service. The working groups each had six to ten members and consulted widely with interested parties. In its findings, the strategy noted that there were significant problems with existing data and information services. These resulted from:

- poor data quality, lack of quality standards or of standard data definitions
- a focus on hospital data and gaps in primary care data
- data accessibility problems and lack of timeliness
- lack of agreed data interchange standards
- a multiplicity of uncoordinated and overlapping data collections
- the high cost of national and AHB information systems
- a poorly maintained National Master Patient Index (Williamson 1991: 3).

Consequently, it was suggested that new data systems, processing, and organisational structures were necessary. Recommendations included that:

- there should be strong links between health sector goals and information systems
- data should be collated once, as close to the source as possible, and used to meet divergent information needs
- national health data should incorporate only data used and validated at a local level
- a national health index (NHI) should be developed, along with a national minimum data set (NMDS) gathering all nationally required data
- a national data dictionary should be developed that defines nationally required data and format rules
- data should be transferred electronically to the NHI and NMDS
- systems should be open to facilitate movement of national applications across platforms
- there should be standard protocols, including national standards and guidelines for data transfer and exchange, to facilitate communication over electronic networks
- private primary care providers should be required to subscribe to national health information systems
- there should be a single national data clearinghouse.

In addition, the strategy recommended establishing a 'National Health Information Service' to manage health information services 'as a business' and take responsibility for resolving some of the problems listed above (Williamson 1991: 5). The goals for the service would be to provide timely and accurate health and related information to a range of 'customers', including the government, the new RHAs, CHEs, and other health agencies. The New Zealand Health Information Service (NZHIS) was thus established in 1992 and commenced a range of projects. These included establishing the NHI and NMDS, and collecting national statistics. With the implementation of the competitive market structures, the new purchasers (RHAs) and providers (CHEs and independent practitioner associations) rapidly sought to develop ICT capacity, and a host of new information requirements began to emerge. While the NZHIS issued a set of broad guidelines for health information systems development (New Zealand Health Information Service 1993), responsibility for coordinating ICT across the health sector was left to the market. This, of course, was in keeping with the government's pro-market philosophy of the time (Bolger, Richardson, and Birch 1990; Boston and Dalziel 1992; Upton 1991).

The competitive era naturally saw the splitting of information collection and management across various agencies. In turn, this amplified the problems that had been highlighted in the 1991 strategy. The NZHIS had been responsible largely for national information services, but had no responsibility for ICT developments, nor for dictating who should be collecting patient, contracting and service information or where this should be deposited. Purchaser and provider agencies collected information for their own purposes, often because counterparts, seeking competitive advantage, refused to share information. Competition appeared to have worked against effective information system development.

By 1996, a range of new agencies, data collections and information interchange systems were in existence. These had various purposes that straddled the different levels of care across public, private and non-government sectors. There were patient information systems that included clinical information, demographic information, and test orders and results. A host of new financial information systems covered public claims, provider invoicing, provider claims, and payment systems.

New administrative systems were required for contract monitoring and statistics. Collecting information in different forms and for different purposes created considerable overlaps in what was collected by different parties. There was no coordination of advice on information policy and issues such as standards for data exchange. There were even problems with fundamentals, such as development of the NHI. There had been no national campaign to educate the public about the aims of the NHI, no concerted effort to obtain provider compliance with NHI requirements, and providers often had difficulty obtaining NHI details for patients from the national database. As a result, it was not uncommon for patients to be assigned more than one NHI number, particularly if they had shifted districts or changed name, and there were a host of 'active' NHI numbers for deceased patients and foreign visitors who happened to have had a health encounter. Such issues complicated processes such as tracking patients and administering service payments, as well as undermining data reliability.

ICT advancements, such as the advent of the web, and changes in policy direction meant that existing systems were becoming outmoded. Following concern that the competitive system had resulted in confusion, complexity and high transaction costs, the government spelled out new directions for health policy, to which information was integral. These included that the health sector should focus on:

- measurable population-based health improvement and identification of groups with poor health status;
- placing people at the centre of health care delivery, requiring portable information and information sharing; and
- getting the greatest amount of services for the dollar through measuring performances, service arrangements, and disseminating best practice guidelines (Shipley 1995).

1996: The Second Ministerial Strategy

In 1996, a second ministerial information strategy was issued. A stocktake undertaken as part of this found:

> a number of areas of concern to the sector, including the fragmented nature of many initiatives and health information systems, the lack of agreed standards and definitions in many areas, and the lack of agreement about access to information by a variety of other parties. Concern was also expressed about the protection of privacy, particularly with increasingly sophisticated use of information technology (Shipley 1996: 4).

The 1996 strategy made several recommendations aimed at resolving the problems outlined above. A Health Information Council was to be created to provide leadership and oversee policy development around standards and governance of health information and ICT. Underpinning the new directions was an assumption that the web would bring together a fragmented sector at low cost (Shipley 1996: 9).

The 1996 election produced the new HFA-led health sector configuration outlined above. This meant the HFA was essentially now responsible for the leadership and coordination of operational matters in the health system, while the Ministry of Health remained responsible for policy development, sector monitoring, and ministerial advice. The restructuring and establishment of the HFA effectively sidelined the development of the Health Information Council and its work programme. Notably, during the amalgamation of the four RHAs into the HFA, little attention was given to information management issues (Health Funding Authority 1999: 22). However, once the HFA had worked through the lengthy and detailed process of establishing itself and its relationships with the health sector, information management and ICT did become a key policy concern and another strategy was developed.

1999: The Third Strategy

In 1999, the HFA issued a 'strategic plan for information and technology management' (Health Funding Authority 1999). The HFA strategy reiterated the problems beleaguering health information and ICT, and noted that information in the health sector was:

> not actively managed to improve quality, quantity, timeliness or purpose of information. This has largely been the result of the former RHA structure and the difficulty of administering sector information in a consistent manner (Health Funding Authority 1999: 9).

Again, the HFA noted the need to coordinate NHI use; formalise management of data collection and key health databases, such as those maintained by the NZHIS and by HFA subsidiaries responsible for reimbursements and contract payments; create formal processes for coordinating information and ICT development within the sector; focus on quality issues; and develop security and privacy guidelines. Furthermore, new funding approaches promoting service integration, budget-holding, and capitation required the collection and interchange of population data in addition to the basic claim data previously collected. The HFA asserted that, with growing dependence on basic data collections and a greater range of data, 'it is with some urgency that the HFA must address data quality and collection' (Health Funding Authority 1999: 10). To do this, the HFA proposed to review and redevelop its own 'business processes and information engines'. These included claims management and payment systems, reporting and monitoring systems and data collection systems. It also proposed developing a data dictionary, and enforcing sector data standards and delivery as a contractual requirement. An application strategy to support the HFA's business processes was designed, along with a structure for information management governance. The HFA strategy listed 73 projects to further investigate a vast array of issues around the organisation and management of data and ICT internal to the HFA (such as that used for 'corporate' strategic planning and decision-making, and service contract management), and across the health sector. These are summarised in Table 3.1 and were scheduled to commence during 1999. The sheer number and range of projects was a direct indication of the poor state of information systems and lack of attention to consolidated planning and development.

In late 1999, the general election produced a change of government and, with this, the third health sector restructuring of the 1990s. The HFA's focus shifted to planning for its own dissolution and redesignation of responsibilities to the Ministry of Health and DHBs. The shift in health sector structures required a new approach for information management and ICT. In May 2000, the HFA and Ministry collaborated on a report that produced a series of recommendations for DHBs and the Ministry

Programme	Aim	Projects
Operating group information management projects	To develop plans and support systems for personal health, public health, Maori health, mental health, and disability support services	23
IT infrastructure	To meet ICT requirements of the HFA	12
Information management and strategic planning	To ensure a consistent approach to information management issues (e.g., NHI, patient databases, etc).	8
Data standards and quality	To provide key decision makers with better quality data shared throughout the sector	4
Implementation of organisational strategy	To implement recommended organisational structures and processes for information management in the HFA	4
Knowledge management and collaboration	To improve HFA's corporate knowledge and methods of exchanging information	4
Transaction systems	To complete implementation of corporate systems, and enhance their use and quality	4
Access to information	To provide key HFA decision makers with access to relevant corporate and sector information	3
Business process improvement	To redesign HFA's business and information processes	3
Business support systems development	To progress availability of adequate business support systems	3
Health sector engagement	To develop consistent information management solutions and standards throughout the sector	3
Data collection and monitoring	To standardise and coordinate data and monitoring processes to improve quality of shared data in the sector	2

Table 3.1. HFA Information Strategy Projects
Source: Adapted from Health Funding Authority (1999: 27–31).

regarding information management capabilities required in the new environment, and the strategies health agencies should adopt to ensure information management and ICT were coordinated, cost-effective, and focused on improving decision-making (Health Funding Authority and Ministry of Health 2000: 2).

Key recommendations included the need to

- develop a set of national information systems based on individual anonymised patient data about health care events
- make these national systems accessible to all agencies involved in managing population health – the Ministry of Health, DHBs, and other providers – via the Health Intranet
- convert existing HFA contracting and payment systems into an application service provider model for use by DHBs and the Ministry.

The report reiterated the host of, by now, long-standing problems with health information and ICT, discussed earlier, that needed to be resolved. To recap, these included sorting out the NHI, developing a National Provider Index (an individual identifier for each service provider), and creating standards for data collection, interchange, security and privacy and for ICT systems. In addition, it was suggested that there was a need to 'create an infrastructure for DHBs and the Health Ministry that is resilient to future sector reform' (Health Funding Authority and Ministry of Health 2000: 7).

Following these recommendations, and acknowledging that a considerable number of information and ICT issues needed to be carefully planned and managed through the transition to the new DHB environment, the Ministry established a high status 'Health Information Management and Technology Plan Advisory Board', chaired by a former Deputy Prime Minister, David Caygill. The project became known as WAVE (Working to Add Value through E-information), and was a concerted effort to reflect on developments over the prior decade of restructuring, develop strategies to address problems, and plan for the future. In many respects, the WAVE project was a rehearsal of the previous information management reviews. But it was also an acknowledgment of the high priority given to 'information' in the new environment. For instance, the enabling *New Zealand Public Health and Disability Act 2000* states that the sector should 'facilitate access to, and the dissemination of, information' to improve all aspects of health care and services. The government's *New Zealand Health Strategy* (King 2001), and a range of other issue-specific strategies designed to guide DHB and provider planning, also highlight the role of information and ICT in improving health care and service integration. A 2005 *Health Information Strategy for New Zealand* (Health Information Strategy Steering Committee 2005) builds upon WAVE's recommendations and developments occurring across the health sector.

Driving the WAVE project were a series of assumptions, reflective of government policy, that:

- all health care providers would be able to access full patient and service delivery information in electronic form via 'open systems'
- health planners would have full and accurate population information and service quality data
- the public would have information about issues including appointment availability, safety of procedures, their rights and choices and the comparative performance of service providers
- software vendors would have an opportunity to help shape national standards along with a strong base to export from.

It was also assumed that, with national planning and coordination, there would be considerable financial savings. These would stem from a consolidated approach to ICT procurement, better service management through reduction of service duplication and overlaps, and improved quality for patients through delivery of more accurate information (WAVE Advisory Board 2001: 11).

In keeping with the plan for an all-encompassing review, the WAVE board was intentionally composed of members from across the health sector and a range of implicated agencies. The findings of the WAVE project were not surprising, particularly in the context of previous reviews and the constant health sector restructuring. The WAVE report listed seventy-nine recommendations. Key recommendations, which differed from those made by the previous reviews discussed earlier, included the establishment of two independent central organisations. One would lead information management policy development, setting of data standards, systems integration, ICT capacity and a host of related issues across the health sector; the other would be responsible for daily business transactions such as paying providers. The rationale for the new agencies was that none of the existing data processing and collection agencies had the capacity to move beyond their daily work to take on a leadership role, they had differing priorities, and there were considerable gaps between and overlaps in their work that needed rectifying (WAVE Organisation Design Project 2001). As noted in the WAVE report, the preference was initially for a single organisation (WAVE Advisory Board 2001: 65). However, the NZHIS was strongly opposed to this as it believed its statistical information functions differed considerably in aim from the 'business' focus of transactions agencies, the 'narrower' requirements of which could raise tolerance for missing or poor data and potentially compromise collection of statistics (WAVE Organisation Design Project 2001: 21). The dual-agency model was, therefore, a trade-off and, in terms of capacity to deliver overall coordination and leadership of health information, was less than ideal.

The most insightful aspect of the WAVE project was not its final report (as indicated, this was largely a rehearsal of previous efforts, designed to place information at the centre of the new policy environment) but the background work and working papers written for the WAVE board by the eight project teams. This work revealed the impact of successive restructurings and the lack of attention through the 1990s to basic information management issues and ICT coordination. For instance, the Systems Architecture Project Team, concerned with ICT development, reported a chaotic state of affairs. It found that messaging systems suffered from:

- no agreed standards due to a 'distinct lack of coordination and leadership right across the sector. The result is that individual organisations, keen to make progress, are adopting messaging schemes that are incompatible' (Systems Architecture Project Team 2001: 26);
- gaps between accepted international standards and requirements. The lack of national agreement on the types of messages required and how they should be formatted had led to 'ongoing ad hoc implementation of the HL7[1] standard in a variety of ways by different parties – which are not fully compatible' (Systems Architecture Project Team 2001: 26);
- a need for greater flexibility to handle both 'push' and 'pull' models of communication;[2]
- an over-reliance on paper-based information interchanges. Many payments, invoicing and clinical information interchanges continued to be in paper form (Systems Architecture Project Team 2001: 27).

Electronic health networks (EHNs), which facilitate the exchange of information, were found to have developed in the absence of a sector-wide strategy. This meant that:

some organisations in the sector, both public and private, have implemented or are looking to implement, their own 'personalised' offering ... What is of concern, and as can be seen across the wider Information Technology community, is that without the adoption and use of agreed sector-wide standards, the ability to exchange information between or across networks will continue to be as difficult to implement in the future, as it is now (Systems Architecture Project Team 2001: 47).

This situation was attributed to:

- lack of promotion of a sector-wide EHN vision. There was no detailed plan for future development, a lack of uptake of sector-wide information exchange, most work had been done on a voluntary basis, developments had been fragmented, not based on any needs analysis and duplicated, and major players in the sector were in disagreement with one another;

- lack of a national EHN framework, raising the prospect that organisations were being tied into customised systems, increasing complexity and cost where organisations would have to engage with 'multiple systems';
- diversity of health care organisations in terms of size, culture, and type, meaning that 'one size fits all' approaches were unlikely to be appropriate;
- lack of agreed standards, meaning systems were competing rather than complementary. This was creating confusion in the sector as to the correct approach, and inducing interfacing problems and waste through purchasing inappropriate technology;
- yet-to-be-realised benefits of the Health Intranet. This was seen by the sector as having high compliance costs and complexity, lacking applications and messaging systems, and not being fully accessible to or supported by the health care community;
- emergence of the public internet as a facilitator of information exchange. However, there was disagreement over its security, performance, and quality (i.e. bandwidth availability, response times between information parties, and likelihood that the network would be available when needed);
- ever-changing technology, complicating choices over technology for provision of an EHN that would be capable of linking with future technologies (Systems Architecture Project Team 2001: 48–52).

The problems with messaging systems and EHNs were matched by difficulties with operational systems. These included the NHI and National Provider Index

Group/agency	Unique systems managed
Ministry of Health	26
NZHIS	20
DHBs	13
Service providers	13
Shared Services Support Group	8
Health Benefits Limited	4
Professional bodies	4
Environmental and Scientific Research	2
Pharmac	2
Births, Deaths and Marriages	1
Department of Work and Income	1
Statistics New Zealand	1
Total	95

Table 3.2. Health Sector Operational Systems
Source: Adapted from Systems Architecture Project Team (2001: 67).

(NPI), required to support integrated care,[3] and administrative systems such as contract management systems and claims validation and processing systems. At least twelve different groups or agencies (possibly more) were maintaining their own operational systems. Each managed a number of unique operational systems as well as using the NHI or NPI (see Table 3.2).

Again, the situation where 'these systems are fragmented across a number of health agencies constraining the delivery of their intended value' (Systems Architecture Project Team 2001: 70) was attributed to the distinct lack of a unified governance system overseeing common business processes. By implication, there were 'multiple systems for the same function', a lack of data linking between NHI and NPI data and contract management data, and a lack of a national view of data: not all health events were captured and there was no consolidated view across the entire health sector – both public and non-government.

The situation with data security, which relies on data encryption and associated policies, was no better. The project team found that:

> few [sector agencies] have the capability to measure how well their security measures are performing. However, one large public hospital reported that they were recording between 40–50 attacks per month by different devices/users. They also indicated this figure is increasing at a steady rate (Systems Architecture Project Team 2001: 76).

The team noted that 128-bit encryption, the highest available standard, was only employed in two instances in the New Zealand health sector. In most cases, 48- and 56-bit encryption, widely recognised as unsatisfactory, was the standard for data transmission, while in some cases there was no encryption. Standards and practices for authenticity (i.e. password usage) were also poor.[4] Again, in only two cases did password requirements meet the minimum of eight alpha-numeric characters. In tandem with this, there was an absence of national security principles, standards and policy, resulting in an inconsistent approach to security issues across the sector. A consequence of this was inadequate and variable protection of health information.

Finally, the project team considered the state of 'data warehousing', or the 'collection of data from a disparate source and systems, that when combined into a formal structure offers more information to the user than the separate individual data elements' (Systems Architecture Project Team 2001: 93). It found a host of problems with existing data warehousing (see Table 3.3).

Table 3.3. (opposite) Data Warehousing Problems
Source: Systems Architecture Project Team (2001: 114–15).

Beyond the WAVE Report

It would be easy to conclude that the WAVE report produced the same findings as the earlier 1991 ministerial strategy. To recap, both found:

- poor data quality
- lack of standards
- gaps in primary care data
- accessibility and information exchange problems
- a lack of coordination between data collections and systems
- problems with national identification systems.

- Missing national datasets (e.g. outpatient, disability support services, GP visits)
- Lack of analytical capacity in policy and funding agencies (ability to extract value from data)
- DHB operational model for contracting with primary care not clear, affecting data requirements and data flows
- Lack of key linking and reference components (i.e. NPI)
- Lack of funding for warehouse developments
- Inability to geo-code transactions due to poor quality or missing data
- Lack of managed infrastructure for access to warehouse data
- Historic concern at cost of using national data
- Lack of data collection, storage and access standards
- Current warehousing architecture may be redundant in DHB environment
- Underdeveloped capacity of source systems to supply necessary data
- Value of information in data warehouses not acknowledged or understood
- Data warehouses under configured and not able to present information when and where needed
- Limited data warehousing experience in the sector
- Poor quality data (e.g. NHI and NPI use)
- Lack of meta-data standards to help develop data interoperability
- No established delivery architecture for warehouse information to be made available to authorised users
- Lack of data compatibility between sources
- Lack of clear governance arrangements
- Case-by-case approach to developing data warehouses

Following such findings, both made comparable recommendations. It seems evident that over a decade, at a strategic policy and development level, the successive restructuring did not assist progress with information management and ICT. However, at the provider and regional level, there were several advancements.

Sector Developments

By at least the mid-1990s, some providers were focusing on ICT as an enabler of more effective service delivery. The Counties Manukau DHB is a prime example. Based in South Auckland, a community known for its low socio-economic status and related high-cost health problems that could be minimised if proactively managed at the community level, the DHB (at that stage a CHE, then a Hospital and Health Service) decided integrated care – linking community providers and the hospital – was the key to reducing hospital service demand. ICT was identified as the facilitator of this, with the hospital taking the developmental lead. Today, the DHB is closely linked with most general practitioners and community providers, as well as with shared electronically accessible databases and messaging systems for a host of clinical and population-based services. Committing to ICT was crucial to this process; equally critical was developing strong working relationships with involved providers. Following several years of system development, the benefits of integration are now starting to emerge. For example, there is evidence that hospital admissions for diabetes-related and other problems have reduced and that child immunisation has increased (Brimacombe 2003; Rowe and Brimacombe 2003). Through the 1990s, independent practitioner associations were also increasingly employing ICT for patient management and profiling, which enabled them to develop population-based health improvement strategies.

Since arrival of the DHB system and the WAVE report, several developments have provided indications of the road ahead. The Ministry of Health has established a Health Sector Information and Technology team dedicated to furthering WAVE recommendations. Much of this team's work involves consulting the health sector around key issues such as security, standards, and systems architecture, as well as developing policy, and supporting and reporting on sector-led developments. A survey of seventeen DHB ICT systems, conducted shortly after the WAVE report, revealed the extent of variation across the country (see Figure 3.1), which might fairly be blamed on the lack of central oversight and coordination through the 1990s. Figure 3.1 portrays the number of different DHB software applications across core DHB information systems. Naturally, this situation presented a host of obstacles to interoperability and related issues that need to be worked through. The many systems beyond DHBs add to the complexity. The Ministry team thus faces a protracted and challenging task. Its role may well be one of mediating between different players and directions, and gently trying to influence behaviour and developments. The Ministry has created a quarterly newsletter, *Health e-News* (available at *www.*

moh.govt.nz/publications), which reports on developments and includes progress reports on WAVE's 'top ten' recommendations (such progress has been limited to date). The Ministry has also looked closely at its own information systems, many of which interface with the broader health sector, and developed a strategic plan to consolidate these.

In 2002, a New Zealand Health Information Standards Organisation was launched to take the 'leadership' role recommended in the WAVE report, while the two existing 'transaction' agencies (the Shared Services Support Group and Health Benefits Limited) were merged to form HealthPAC (Health Payments, Agreements and Compliance). HealthPAC work may eventually be conducted via a health portal, while subscription to the Health Intranet, a portal precursor, continues to grow. The NZHIS remains an independent unit within the Ministry of Health dedicated to data collection. It has launched an 'Infostructure Programme', which aims to establish ICT systems that provide the health sector with access to NZHIS databases. This programme also includes upgrading the NHI by removing the approximately 800,000 'duplicate' entries and extending NHI electronic access to primary care providers, and establishing a Health Practitioner Index that identifies all registered health practitioners by a single number. Beyond central agencies and, to a degree, outside of their influence, the chief information officers of DHBs have been regularly meeting to discuss issues and strategy; a number of independent

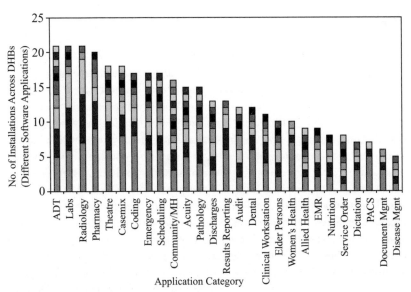

Figure 3.1: Installations of Software Packages.
Note: Where installation numbers in the figure do not correspond with the number of DHBs (21) data is either missing or electronic systems are not installed.

practitioner association information managers are also working together to ensure that their patient management systems are compatible and support interoperability.

There are a burgeoning number of sector-driven collaborative ICT projects, including inter-regional and integrated care initiatives. The information functions of the three Auckland-based DHBs have been merged, facilitating the sharing of hospital and community data and the extension of the Counties Manukau integrated care ICT initiative. Elsewhere, similar ICT mergers and interoperability projects are in process, but these tend to be based on specific services or are between selected DHBs (Health Information Strategy Steering Committee 2005: 62). For example, the Wellington independent practitioner association has developed an ICT-enabled service integration which facilitates retinal screening of diabetics by community optometrists, circumventing the need for referral to a hospital-based ophthalmologist (Love 2003). The Ministry and several DHB hospitals have negotiated a common price for access to fulltext medical knowledge databases such as OVID; the Southland DHB has provided practitioners external to the hospital with online access to these, while the others have made them internally available (Ministry of Health 2002: 67). Hospitals are beginning to install web-enabled intranets for accessing and transmitting clinical information, and electronic prescribing systems are becoming more common. DHBs are focusing on reducing the number of software vendors they deal with to induce greater national consistency. Meanwhile, more than 20 software companies have formed the New Zealand Health IT Cluster with the intention of aligning the work of its members more closely with health sector requirements, and coordinating international marketing efforts (see *www.healthit.org.nz*).

Governance and Institutional Arrangements

The landscape described in this chapter is bewildering and multifaceted, making it difficult to discern the relative positions of its many players: government, the various central health information agencies, DHBs and other non-government health care providers, and private IT companies. This situation complicates the working out of what the road ahead might look like. In addition, a lack of clarity over the 'institutional arrangements'– the structures and norms that govern policymaking and organisation – has surfaced. Clearly, there is no singular health information leader in New Zealand's health sector; on the contrary, leadership and policy appears to come from several sources, as noted in the 2005 health information strategy (Health Information Strategy Steering Committee 2005). The positive side of this pluralism is that the capacity for moving in a direction that could result in massive failure (as in the case of INCIS described in Chapter 5) may be reduced. On the negative side, however, strong leadership and building of a consensus over directions may, following the rocky road of the 1990s, be just what is needed. Certainly, the WAVE report and the reviews that preceded it highlighted the need for central control and oversight. However, without political commitment, this may be difficult to achieve in the present environment.

In terms of the framework that will govern health information management and IT in the foreseeable future, it could be suggested that there will be incremental advancement across sometimes isolated, loosely or closely connected developments. Many developments will be driven by collaborative activity within the sector itself, which is the approach promoted in the government's 2005 strategy (Health Information Strategy Steering Committee 2005). The 2005 strategy provides a 'bird's-eye' view of the possible path ahead, namely that:

- most information (for example, patient records) will be collected and shared at the local level by Primary Health Organisations and DHBs
- some population and planning information will be collected and held regionally, across DHBs
- some will be nationally maintained.

Collaboration and interoperability are, again, the keys to this structure, as are yet-to-be-created 'stewardship' arrangements (Health Information Strategy Steering Committee 2005: 49–51).

Developments across the sector will continue to be increasingly monitored, supported where relevant and, in some cases, compelled by central agencies through contractual requirements. As noted, an enduring element of the funding of public health care in New Zealand since the 1990s has been the formal contract negotiated between funder and provider. A potential advantage of this is the ability to propel providers in centrally driven contract-specified directions. With increasing inclusion of information delivery requirements in contracts, and the application of centrally derived ICT policy strategy, there is growing capacity for the centre to influence sector-wide ICT developments. However, for progress toward interoperability to continue, the centre needs a highly developed and coordinated ICT strategy that is widely recognised and supported; the input of ICT system and policy experts will also be crucial in contract negotiations. As illustrated in this chapter, only the foundations of such a scenario have been laid. At best, it may be several years before New Zealand reaches a point where systems are fully integrated and interoperable.

Conclusion

This chapter reviewed the impact that New Zealand's decade of health-sector restructuring and shifting policy preferences has had on health care information management and ICT development. It suggests that, in the absence of central oversight of ICT developments, or a clearly developed policy to which government demonstrates a strong and enduring commitment, the result is multiplicity of divergent systems. For this, New Zealand's political leaders, fixated through the 1990s and into the new millennium on health system structure, are largely to blame. Of course, their failure to give consideration to effective health information governance arrangements through the restructuring period has undermined the present quest for interoperability – a fundamental requirement for those seeking service integration, cross-sectoral collaboration, and data sharing. Another result has been pluralistic governance arrangements, which have both advantages and disadvantages.

Clearly, a key lesson from the New Zealand example is that, if interoperability is desired, then there is a very real role for central governance and regulation. Included in this is the development and enforcement of standards for ICT system architecture and for data collection, security, and transfer. This must be coupled with the promotion of an ICT strategy and support to implicated parties (the many organisations involved in health care delivery) for its development. Experience elsewhere with developing effective health information systems also suggests a role for central control and incentives (Casilino *et al.* 2003).

As discussed in this chapter, the New Zealand government has latterly sought to boost capacity for health information governance. Given the preceding history of ICT developments, and considerable investment across the health sector in existing infrastructure, it faces an uphill struggle. In the meantime, work is required in three areas. The first involves rectifying problems associated with the restructuring era and shift from competition to coordination, including dealing with the many overlapping databases, data collection inconsistencies, and lack of information coordination across the health sector. The second is the need to update incompatible systems, particularly databases and systems used for financial and administrative transactions, patient record management, and clinical work. The third is the demand to deal with complex organisational, planning and policy issues such as the development of national systems architecture guidelines, security and privacy policy, the creation of a coherent and functional institutional basis for the development of sound policy and coordination of ICT, and consolidation of information strategies.

The continual advance of ICT complicates these tasks, as will further policy changes. New Zealand's experience implies that, in a highly politicised, disaggregated, and transient environment, developing and implementing health sector ICT strategies is far from straightforward. Moreover, repetitive restructuring and shifting policy are detrimental to information management and ICT development, particularly in the absence of well-developed strategic plans or of comprehensive central oversight. Although New Zealand's recent history of restructuring may be unique, its transition from a market-oriented to collaborative health service environment matches that of other developed countries. For this reason, the difficulties with health care information management and ICT development observed in New Zealand might be expected elsewhere.

4.

A Major Health Care Information
System Project Failure

In the late 1990s, two of New Zealand's larger public hospital organisations, Health
Waikato Ltd (HW) and Capital Coast Health Ltd (CCH), purchased new information
systems from Shared Medical Systems (SMS), a North American company. In both
the HW and CCH cases, the promises of the new SMS system were considerable. In
both, implementation of the new systems failed, resulting in a waste of taxpayer money.
Implementation was beset with problems from the outset, particularly so at HW. The
SMS system had been only partially installed at HW, but not running, at the time it was
abandoned in May 2000, merely eighteen months from the date the system had been
purchased. The financial cost to HW was reported to have been at least $17 million. At
CCH, SMS was partly functional until being finally laid to rest in 2003 at a cost of around
$26 million.

This chapter reviews the HW case. As this was linked to the CCH purchase, the
chapter briefly outlines developments at CCH. In both cases, the issue was larger than
simply the failure of an information system. It was a story that:

- shows how a governing board and senior management decision-makers managed to
  purchase a system that quite possibly was the wrong one
- portrays considerable shortcomings in the process of planning and decision-making
  for a large-scale, publicly-funded project
- involves highly complex decision-making and planning
- involves a wide range of players, including government, industry, business
  consultants, hospital management, the hospital governing board, IT specialists,
  health care workers, politicians, and the media
- leaves in its wake a tangled path of events
- illustrates how the magnitude of an apparently straightforward decision to purchase
  a new health information system can be easily misunderstood
- demonstrates that information systems are not easily 'bolted onto' organisations.
  Implementation is a substantial undertaking, with many unforeseen difficulties,
  requiring considerable organisational adaptation
- exemplifies how, apparently, no one is to blame for failure. Several events and issues,

each of which is contested, appear to have been contributing factors
- provides a number of critical lessons for health care information technology planners and public sector governance.

The discussions that follow are based on an analysis of several thousand pages of documents obtained under New Zealand's Official Information Act from the Ministry of Health, Crown Company Monitoring Advisory Unit, HW, and CCH. Included were reports, correspondence, and meeting minutes. The chapter firstly overviews the SMS company and system. Secondly, it details the HW experience. Finally, the key lessons are summarised.

The Technology: Shared Medical Systems

At the time of the HW and CCH purchases, the North American SMS was one of the world's two largest health care information system suppliers. It employed around 6500 people, with around 3500 customers in twenty countries. Its primary market was North America, and it was keen to move into the Australasian market. An SMS New Zealand branch was established in 1997, around the time of the CCH purchase. In late-2000, SMS was taken over by Siemens Corporation, the United States division of German company AG Siemens. SMS withdrew from New Zealand in 2001.

Health information systems are required for various functions such as the management of operating theatres, laboratory services, pharmaceuticals, patients and finance. Such information systems routinely function independently from one another, with minimal interoperability, due to the fact that in any one hospital some systems are developed 'in house' while others will be purchased from vendors. By contrast, the SMS suite offered an integrated suite of products with the promise of full interoperability among the various components. The client might, therefore, expect SMS to provide for its complete information management needs.

The SMS product purchased by HW and CCH consisted of a series of independent 'modules' serving various of the above-mentioned purposes. Core modules included:

- 'Allegra'. This offered: a patient administration system for invoicing; a medical records system for registering and tracking of inpatients and outpatients; a clinical decision support system with electronic ordering of laboratory and radiology services; clinical coding of medical conditions; and mental health management
- 'eCR', or electronic clinical records
- 'MRS', or multi-resource scheduling
- 'BEV', or business executive view. This offered data warehousing including basic patient data from Allegra for patient costing, and key performance indicator and financial reports
- Health care clinical guidelines to assist with best medical practice and patient pathways through the hospital.

In addition, SMS offered a basic information services platform that would be regularly updated, in keeping with new developments. SMS also was capable of linking with other information system products because of the 'open' nature of the software. Thus, as an 'off-the-shelf' package, SMS presented an attractive option for large hospital organisations seeking integrated information management. This stated, implementation of the SMS suite was not an insubstantial undertaking. It meant complete replacement of existing information systems, training of IT staff and users across the recipient organisation, and organisational re-engineering in terms of how clinical and administrative staff would use IT, and the additional effort needed to input new data required by the SMS system.

Health Waikato Ltd and SMS

The HW experience was one surrounded with controversy. First, through the SMS process, which commenced in early 1997 and ended in mid-2000, there were several resignations of key staff members including the chief executive and other closely involved senior management. For much of the time there was no chief information officer to lead the project. In the absence of senior management, the HW board chair and other board members engaged in HW decision-making over the SMS purchase that would normally be the work of the chief executive and chief information officer. The SMS purchase decision was apparently pushed through by the board chair, without the full scrutiny or endorsement of the board and HW management and clinical staff. Second, a high profile HW board member resigned, citing opposition to SMS as a contributing factor. This spurred a series of investigations, demanded by the Minister of Health and CCMAU,[1] into the SMS purchase. Third, there was close political involvement, including allegations that then Minister of Health, Bill English, had influenced the board's decision to buy SMS, and involvement of ministerial representatives such as CCMAU in the decision-making process. Fourth, it was never clear that SMS would be able to deliver on HW's information system needs, or that HW's needs were ever defined. In fact, evidence emerged early in the negotiation process of ill-defined needs, of shortcomings in the SMS product, and of utility in retaining the existing HW information system. Despite this, the purchase still took place. The purchase process was then subject to review even before any implementation of the SMS product occurred. Fifth, it took almost two years to work through the process of deciding to contract with SMS. Throughout this time, several options were considered, with new concerns constantly arising, and questions raised over SMS's appropriateness. Sixth, the case received much media coverage due to the considerable cost involved in the SMS purchase, but also as disagreements over the SMS system between HW staff, management, and the board surfaced.

Information Systems Prior to SMS

To understand how HW ended up with the SMS system it is necessary to trace developments prior to the December 1998 purchase. The story commenced in 1993, when a market model of health system organisation had just been implemented in New Zealand (Gauld 2000). Information on service costs and throughput was a key requirement of the competitive tendering and contracting arrangements that underscored health service funding. The corporate organisational structure applied also required the HW hospitals, spread across several sites, to share and combine information.

Against this background, in June 1994, HW entered into partnership with Fujitsu to provide a patient management system known as Hospro-W (hereafter referred to as Hospro). This included several standard hospital modules that Fujitsu was to develop specifically for HW. Hospro was to be fully implemented by 1996. However, there were 'a number of problems' noted with Fujitsu's performance and commitment to the Hospro project, including cost overruns, project delays, and an apparent lack of urgency on Fujitsu's part. Consequently, the completion date was delayed until 1997 (Health Waikato Ltd 1997d: 1). Moreover, Hospro had not provided HW with the anticipated degree of flexibility, performance or user friendliness. There had been difficulties with functionality across multiple sites, adding and modifying fields, questioning the database, and generating ad hoc reports. HW was also the only Hospro user in New Zealand, a situation with which it was uncomfortable (Health Waikato Ltd 1997d: 2).

By the mid-1990s, government health policy around how to provide effective health services had shifted to embrace service integration, facilitated by information technology (Shipley 1995; 1996). This said, in this period, the government generally took a 'hands off' role in information technology planning and other Crown Health Enterprise (CHE) decisions. Following government policy, the HW board and management developed a broad strategic vision for health service delivery, although this was far from a detailed practical IT strategy. The vision was to provide seamless care, throughout a patient's life, regardless of geographic location (Health Waikato Ltd 1997d). Underpinning the vision, of course, was the need for an information system that would provide electronic patient records and support integration (Health Waikato Ltd 1997a; Health Waikato Ltd 1997c). In sum, HW was eager to replace Hospro, and install a system used by other CHEs that would support the new vision. To this end, in early 1997, the HW board and management resolved to commence a search for alternatives (Jenkins n.d.). Shortly after, a group of HW representatives travelled to the United Kingdom and United States where they visited IT suppliers Irish Medical Systems, Atwork, Moores and SMS.

Enter SMS: The Link with CCH

In July 1997, SMS appeared on HW's procurement agenda as the favoured option, following a HW visit to CCH to view the SMS system. CCH was under the interim executive chairmanship of HW Chair Jack Jenkins, who had been brought in to sort out financial and managerial problems with the organisation. CCH had purchased SMS in December 1996, in questionable circumstances. The purchase was essentially led by Jenkins, who had met with Dr Leo Mercer, a Texas physician and SMS consultant, at a presentation in the United States. Following the United States meeting, in early 1997, Mercer was appointed chief executive of CCH. Media reports suggested he was paid two salaries, one of around $300,000 as chief executive, and another of $178,000 as a consultant for SMS (New Zealand Press Association 1999a). As such, there was also a suggestion of a conflict of interest between Mercer's role with SMS and the CCH purchase. An Audit Office investigation later cleared Mercer from any wrongdoing (Controller and Auditor-General 1999). As a champion of SMS, and experienced with its systems, Mercer was seen as crucial to driving the SMS implementation and organisational re-engineering required (Jackson and Keane 1999: 15).

By the time of the initial July 1997 HW visit, SMS implementation at CCH had only just commenced. It subsequently emerged that there were several problems at CCH with SMS. First, the pre-purchase evaluation of SMS was not as detailed as it could have been, and the decision to purchase was 'fast tracked'. Second, only North American systems were considered for purchase. Third, there was a lack of documentation around how board decisions were made, and not all board meetings about IT purchases were fully attended. Moreover, while Jenkins, in his role as executive chairman, acted within delegated authority in single-handedly negotiating the SMS contract, it would have been desirable to have involved the board in such a large and significant purchase (Controller and Auditor-General 1999: 44–5). Fourth, the SMS version delivered to CCH was different from that demonstrated to clinical staff. The board's preference was for a 'tried and true' version, rather than a newer version preferred by clinical staff. Furthermore, there was a lack of clinical support for the system. As the Auditor-General noted:

> Clinical ownership, buy-in and commitment, in their fullest sense, have not been achieved. The system has introduced a level of management control and accountability that was not in place with previous systems. It is fair to say that the primary purpose of some modules is to collect management information as opposed to providing direct assistance to the user in the performance of their job (Controller and Auditor-General 1999: 39).

Fifth, there were many staff complaints about SMS functionality and support. These included: failure by SMS to fix problems in a timely manner; information not being presented in a user-friendly format; some processes being unnecessarily complex; the system not being as 'integrated' as claimed; and a lack of capacity to deliver customised reports (Controller and Auditor-General 1999: 36–7). Sixth, there were problems in launching system components, some of which were ultimately discarded, fuelling negativities about SMS among staff and health workforce unions (New Zealand Press Association 1999d). In the end, only part of the system was ever implemented due to difficulties with modifying software for New Zealand settings (Guysan 2000). Seventh, Leo Mercer departed in mid-1999, barely two years after his arrival. This left the SMS implementation without a champion. The system continued to be supported by subsequent management but the SMS project remained troubled. The package being installed was neither integrated nor comprehensive, with pharmacy, radiology and other services provided by alternative information system suppliers. The decision to replace SMS was announced in October 2003 (Association of Salaried Medical Specialists 2003). Since then, CCH has continued to experience information system difficulties including cost overruns, project delays, and system 'outages' (MacDonald 2004).

The HW SMS Purchase Process

In late July 1997, following the HW board visit to CCH, a paper written for the HW board comparing the various alternatives recommended 'that Health Waikato Limited become a partner with Capital Coast Health and SMS in implementation of SMS software solutions' (Health Waikato Ltd 1997d: 5). The estimated purchase cost was $14.86 million, plus $3.25 million for switching to SMS from Hospro (Health Waikato Ltd 1997d: 4). On 3 August, in the absence of a chief information officer, HW commissioned a report by the Hunter Group, an IT consultant, on its IT strategic plan and SMS preference. This supported HW's decisions, but questioned whether the organisation was ready and capable of implementing the SMS project (Hunter Group 1997). This ought to have sounded a caution to the HW board, particularly given the events that followed. However, at its 7 August meeting, the board agreed to enter into negotiation with SMS. It also resolved that financial and implementation plans contained in the board paper, which detailed a staged and complex process designed by CCH, form the basis of the negotiations with SMS to be undertaken by HW Chief Executive, Garry Smith. Finally, the board recommended that a chief information officer be 'appointed immediately' along with the convening of project steering and review groups, led by HW finance and audit manager, Ben Smit (Health Waikato Ltd 1999a). The chief information officer post was, however, never filled during the entire SMS negotiation and installation process; instead, the project was advised and guided by a series of consultants (Health Waikato Ltd Board 1999). According to later media coverage, Smit was apparently uncomfortable with the entire process surrounding the SMS decision, suggesting that many of the reports he prepared for the board were not properly evaluated. He eventually resigned from HW for fear that his professional reputation might otherwise be destroyed (Pepperell 2000).

HW spent August and September 1997 studying SMS and its implementation more closely. It was here that concerns about SMS first emerged. At least one independent report, by Deloitte and Touche Consulting Group, was commissioned and an independent IT adviser stated that HW should not sign any SMS contract (Health Waikato Ltd 1999b). The Deloitte's report (Deloitte and Touche Consulting Ltd 1997) found that:

> SMS's proposal is based for the most part on US sourced packaged software (p.4) ... part of HWL's strategy for SMS implementation is to install the standard products plus NZ-essential modifications and to fit the business to the software (p.11) ... The documentation seen by us does not clearly identify what is included within 'New Zealand modifications' (p.4) ... We have not been able to determine in our discussions with HWL personnel what scope of work is being proposed by SMS, or what SMS requires of the buyer (p.13) ... No allowance appears to have been made by either party for the change management effort required to implement clinical systems such as the [electronic medical record] (p.13).

A report on findings from the study period, *Health Waikato Limited: Clinical Information Systems Plan*, was prepared by Ben Smit (Health Waikato Ltd 1997a). HW Chair Jack Jenkins requested this not be presented to the board (Health Waikato Ltd 1999a). The report noted that the 7 August recommendation to proceed with SMS 'was made on the basis of several premises some of which are now in question' (Health Waikato Ltd 1997a: 1). These included that:

> (1) Functionality of SMS can demonstrate a complete, working integrated solution which meets our needs.

> A comparison of Business functionality [of SMS] is not as close as was first thought and particularly in the areas of mental health, community health, theatre management, histopathology and chart tracking are not a good fit with expected requirements. Some other applications have only a partial fit with requirements. [This leaves HW] very open to not achieving the Business needs of the system.

> (2) SMS's solution is compatible with our current hardware configuration.
> Extensive investigation has been undertaken over the last two months and the current proposal indicates an additional capital requirement of $3.1 million. This additional capital does not include the costs of Stage 4 (Medical and Document Imaging, etc).

(3) SMS is no more costly than continuing to develop the Hospro-W system.
Capital costs will be $11.4 million higher than our current allowance for Clinical
Information Systems. Interest and operating costs add $7.6 million to cash outlays and
make the total cash outlay difference between the two options of $19 million... $15.8
million higher than our current Business Plan (Health Waikato Ltd 1997a: 4–5).

The report recommended that the SMS project not be implemented. Instead, HW
should develop an updated information systems plan describing the IT needs of the
company, justifying the approach taken, and providing an implementation plan that
would 'deliver solutions'. The resulting project, from October to November 1997,
was called 'Info 2000+'. Again, led by Smit, this had a wide-ranging membership
drawn from management and clinical staff and produced terms of reference to
guide any HW information system developments (Health Waikato Ltd 1997e).
The project also investigated four IT companies as potential 'strategic information
partners': SMS, Cerner, CSC/HBOC, and Fujitsu. In November 1997, a request for
information was sent to each, along with a request for a proposal. In December 1997,
each of the four companies made presentations to HW. Info 2000+ then produced
a report recommending the Australian Cerner as the preferred partner in a joint IT
Strategic and Implementation Planning Study, and that SMS be given opportunity to
resubmit their proposal should Cerner not meet HW's expectations (Health Waikato
Ltd 1997b). The HW board's response was to resolve that further study of *both*
Cerner and SMS was required, the study of the latter being due to its New Zealand
presence at CCH.

In February 1998, a board subcommittee along with HW management and
clinicians visited hospitals in Australia and the United States to study Cerner and
SMS. From then to October 1998, there was ongoing discussion over whether to
select Cerner or SMS. Management and clinical staff favoured Cerner; the board
appeared uncertain (Jenkins n.d.) and possibly in favour of SMS. Cerner's technology
was allegedly much more advanced than SMS's, but consequently carried more risk.
Concerns about Y2K compliance were also being raised more consistently, along
with concerns about capacity for either Cerner or SMS to provide a total solution.
Cerner's patient administration system had only been employed in one Australian
hospital.

In May, the board discussed another options paper prepared by HW management
(Health Waikato Ltd 1998c). This again recommended partnership with Cerner.
However, again, the board was not convinced, requesting further presentations by
both Cerner and SMS. It also requested another consultant's report, this time by
Optimation. In May and June, SMS gave two presentations to the HW board.

By the time the Optimation report was delivered in September, urgency was
creeping into the decision-making process. Optimation's report suggested that SMS
carried less risk, and was therefore preferable but not ideal, recommending any

decision to opt for SMS be delayed by three months to 'observe implementation of SMS at CCH and of Cerner in New South Wales' (Jenkins n.d.; Optimation New Zealand 1998). Also in September, HW Chief Executive Garry Smith delivered a paper that was the first to contain a HW clinician needs analysis, or to address the issue of clinical buy-in. This recommended another option of interfacing the Hospro patient administration system with Cerner's clinical applications, with movement to Cerner's patient administration system within two years. The paper argued that this option had strong clinical buy-in, offered advanced technology, Australasian presence, phased installation, would be user-friendly and easier to manage from an IT department perspective (Health Waikato Ltd 1998a). Fujitsu also wrote to the board confirming its support for Hospro through future developments.

At its 30 September meeting, following a now familiar pattern, and siding with the Optimation advice, the board recommended that no decision on a partner could be made at that point in time. Also, the board recommended that management address concerns of board members, which included evaluating the relative risk of Cerner (a new product) vis-à-vis SMS (a more 'mature' product) along with Y2K compliance (Health Waikato Ltd 1999a; Jenkins n.d.). It was clear that, by now, the contrast between the perspectives of management and the board was growing. As board chair, Jack Jenkins, later wrote in a letter to CCMAU, underscoring this were, 'external priorities', namely:

> Shareholding Ministers' preference for the implementation of 'package solutions' rather than 'in-house information systems'. In other words, Health Waikato's shareholders wished for it to invest in Information Technology which is broadly consistent across the public health sector; this could include liaising with other public health providers (Jenkins 1998).

This view had previously been conveyed in meetings and in at least two letters to Jack Jenkins, on 19 October and 13 November, from Andrew Weeks of CCMAU. Weeks wrote that he was 'very concerned' about HW's possible 'in-house' preference for Cerner and Hospro:

> I would draw your attention to the business planning meeting with the Minister earlier this year, where he made it clear that Government favours packaged solutions and a movement away from bespoke systems that have been developed wholly or partially in-house. The government has an unenviable recent history of major investments in bespoke software with a minimal degree of success. From time to time CCMAU is approached for advice on how to address the complexities of IT in the hospital sector. Our response is consistent and centres around a strategy that replaces bespoke systems with un-customised packaged software solutions ... I understand that the board is meeting for a strategic planning session and would be grateful if you would

communicate my concerns about the mixed messages over the IT strategy; and advise me of the confirmed IT strategy so that I can apprise the Minister accordingly (Weeks 1998).

From October through December 1998, a series of significant events took place as the board shifted its weight in favour of SMS following the ministerial 'advice' outlined above. On 13 October, Garry Smith resigned as HW Chief Executive, receiving a severance payment of up to $185,000 (Mold 1999). Due to his contractual agreement with HW, he was unable to state the reason for his resignation. However, reports received by journalists suggested Smith was concerned that the SMS system, which he did not support, would be purchased (Mold 1998; Pepperell 2000). On 14 October, senior clinical staff wrote to Board Deputy Chair Max Lamb stating their opposition to SMS and that 'the future of any hospital information system hinges on the buy-in of the clinical staff who must use it' (Health Waikato Ltd 1999b; Pepperell 2000). Just prior to a 16 October board strategic planning retreat in Taupo, Andrew Weeks' above-mentioned letter, requesting an IT decision, was received. The day after the retreat, a board delegation visited CCH to view the SMS system.

On 19 October, the board convened a special meeting to appoint an acting chief executive, Brad Healy. Healy was directed to make IT a 'number one priority' (Jenkins 1998) and to undertake further study of the options with the assistance of external consultants: status quo with Y2K updates; SMS; or Cerner (laboratory and radiology only) with Hospro. The study was to 'include consideration of the strategic benefits to be gained from a risk minimisation perspective of adopting the same information system platform already used by another tertiary hospital' (Jenkins 1998).

The next board meeting, chaired by Max Lamb in Jack Jenkins' absence, was convened on 28 October. At this meeting, which followed a Y2K meeting, the board recommended that any IT partner selection be deferred until after 2000 (Health Waikato Ltd 1999a). On 30 October, David Wickham, chair of the board's IT subcommittee, wrote to Lamb expressing Jenkins' disappointment at the board's failure to select an IT partner (Health Waikato Ltd 1999b).

On 23 November 1998, merely four weeks after commencing the options study, Brad Healy presented *Information Systems – Future Direction* to the board (Health Waikato Ltd 1998b). This recommended SMS on the basis that:

- it fitted with the government's IT philosophy as outlined by Andrew Weeks above
- the board's preference was for a standardised product
- there were advantages of having a system used by another New Zealand hospital (Health Waikato Ltd 1998b: 5–6).

The report and the minutes of the board meeting held only one day after its delivery, at which the report's recommendation was endorsed, show that there remained several reservations about SMS and the decision-making process:

- Concerns existed about the capacity and willingness of HW to cope with the changes required to implement SMS.
- Clinical staff continued to have concerns about SMS, although those who had visited CCH apparently were 'quite happy with the SMS system' (Health Waikato Ltd Board 1998).
- HW would continue to carry the risk of any SMS implementation failures.
- SMS required a reduction in IT staff at HW from twenty-nine to around fifteen. The board noted that IT staff would need to be actively involved in SMS implementation or they would be 'naturally resistant to the change' (Health Waikato Ltd Board 1998).
- Some board members expressed concerns over the 'opportunity cost' of the required capital spending and the timing of the report, in that they had had insufficient time (one day) to consider the recommendations. The board rejected the idea that an option of not signing a final purchase contract should be included in an agreement with SMS for the planning and implementation phase. There continued to be concerns about the tight implementation timetable, with SMS to be fully operable by 2000.

Despite the above, the board agreed to enter into a contract to purchase and implement SMS clinical applications. It directed that SMS contractually confirm that its systems were Y2K compliant and would interface with other systems at HW, and that the contract be structured in a way that would allow HW to determine the implementation timetable. Max Lamb voted against the resolution (Health Waikato Ltd Board 1998). On 16 December 1998, the SMS contract was signed by a HW board representative. By that time the purchase process had already been subject to significant external scrutiny and controversy.

HW Purchases SMS Amid Questioning

HW announced its purchase decision in a 26 November 1998 press release (Health Waikato Ltd 1998d). On the same day, the story made the front page of the *Waikato Times*, which reported that 'several senior medical staff have told *The Times* that they don't want the SMS system. They say the current system could be improved and that money should instead be spent on frontline care'. The story also quoted Acting Chief Executive Brad Healy as saying the HW board and management were 'mindful of the benefit of obtaining a system which is already in place at another major hospital and health service ... which will enable us to have the backup we currently don't have ... it is timely to invest in a proven system that can take us forward' (Mold 1998). The purchase also made the *New Zealand Herald*, which suggested the price had 'appalled medical staff who say the hospital is paying millions for a "marginal" increase in technology instead of putting money into frontline care'. The New Zealand Nurses Organisation and Association of Salaried Medical Specialists were also reported as being upset at the decision, particularly because the views of frontline staff had been disregarded (Gardner 1998; Howard 1998).

Prior to 26 November, questions had been raised in Parliament about SMS and issues surrounding the decision-making process, particularly the possibility of collusion between Jenkins, Andrew Weeks, CCH Chief Executive Leo Mercer, and SMS. Health Minister Bill English's response was standard: the decision-making process was an operational matter and not the Minister's responsibility (New Zealand Parliamentary Debates, 12 November 1998). However, the questions were forwarded to Jack Jenkins by CCMAU, the shareholding Ministers' representative, concerned that due process had been followed and requesting advice on the 'contract processes and procedures' for IT purchases by HW (Anderson 1998). On 27 November, Alliance Health Spokesperson Phillida Bunkle launched an attack on the purchase process and SMS system, suggesting 'unanimous rejection' by clinical staff, serious deficiencies with SMS, and collusion between 'senior bureaucrats' in the purchase process, adding that 'I have been told that Mr. Jenkins and Mr. Mercer (of CCH) recently held a meeting in Arizona with the departing head of the Government's Crown-company monitor CCMAU, Andrew Weekes [sic]. I want to know if the SMS system was discussed at that meeting' (Bunkle 1998). Bunkle also announced that she was writing to Health Minister Bill English, asking a series of questions. These included whether independent studies confirmed that SMS was the best system for HW; and whether the Minister was satisfied over the role of Jenkins, Weeks, and Mercer in the purchase process (Bunkle 1998).

In the following weeks, political scrutiny of the SMS purchase process escalated with a series of communications between the Minister, CCMAU, and the HW board. CCMAU file notes reported the board 'split' over the SMS decision, that Max Lamb had implied the questions raised in the public arena about SMS performance and acceptability were legitimate (Crown Company Monitoring Advisory Unit 1998b), and that the paper trail leading to the SMS decision was far from complete (Crown Company Monitoring Advisory Unit 1998a). Jack Jenkins was then asked to outline the steps in the process and rationale for key decisions (Jenkins n.d.). In late December, the board negotiated a pause in the SMS contract. This effectively delayed implementation, but meant that the SMS purchase of software applications and license fees went ahead as planned.

On 18 January 1999, Max Lamb resigned from the HW board, further politicising the purchase process. In his resignation letters to the Health Minister and the board, Lamb cited several concerns, including that his views were contrary to those of the Minister, as relayed via Andrew Weeks, and the implication the HW board would be removed if a new IT system were not in place by 2000. Therefore, he believed it was 'not appropriate' to remain a board member. However, Lamb's primary concern was:

The major issue for me has been the SMS decision ... I have been, and am opposed, to the decisions because of the risk (particularly Y2K), management credibility, and process, or rather a lack of process, factors. Notwithstanding the negotiation of a pause in the contract, I am very concerned at the pressures which the decision will make on the organisation (Lamb 1999).

Around the same time, Labour Health Spokesperson Annette King wrote to the Audit Office requesting a review of the SMS decision. This was declined as the Audit Office only had the powers to examine the 'effectiveness and efficiency' with which hospitals used resources (New Zealand Press Association 1999c). However, Lamb's resignation did lead to an investigation into the matter by CCMAU who found that '[the HW] Chair appears to have misinterpreted the views conveyed to him by [CCMAU] with regard to the Minister's wishes on IT solutions and Y2K compliance' (Crown Company Monitoring Advisory Unit 1999: 7). Furthermore, 'some process issues' required further investigation. CCMAU and the HW chair agreed to an independent assurance review of the SMS process, funded by HW (Crown Company Monitoring Advisory Unit 1999). This, combined with pressure from Opposition politicians, led to the July 1999 engagement of consultants Bell Gully. By this time, HW had appointed a new chief executive, Dr Jan White. A budget of $120,000 was provided for the review (White 1999), the scope of which was limited to 'the process of decision making, not a review of the final decision [to select SMS] itself' (Health Waikato Ltd 1999c).

The Bell Gully team reviewed documents and interviewed HW staff and board members involved in the SMS purchase. An interim consultation report was circulated for response in August 1999. The Bell Gully study, of course, was flanked by a series of further commissioned studies and opinions on the SMS purchase. The Audit Office, for instance, provided information on the costs to date of the SMS purchase, estimated to be around $9.2 million plus a further $1.39 million per year in support fees (Audit New Zealand 1999). Following concerns about cost increases and SMS performance, the HW management team, led by Jan White, requested legal opinion on the SMS contract. Legal advisers Chapman Tripp wrote that the 'scope of deliverables' was loosely defined and lacking detail, leaving HW in a vulnerable position. Furthermore, that 'while Health Waikato believed it was to be supplied with a New Zealand model that would only require minimal "nationalisation", SMS now indicates that its "US model" will be provided. You will require significant customisation work, some of which may be at Health Waikato's expense' (Chapman Tripp 1999). Australian IT consultants, Simsion Bowles, were also commissioned by HW, delivering several reports.

Just prior to delivery of Bell Gully's final report, the 1999 general election delivered a new Labour-led coalition government with Annette King as health minister. On Tuesday 21 December 1999, the final Bell Gully report was delivered. The preceding

Friday, Jack Jenkins resigned as HW chair. He subsequently stated the Bell Gully report had nothing to do with his resignation; that a change of government and health policy direction meant it was time for a new leadership (New Zealand Press Association 1999b). Bell Gully's (1999) principal findings were that:

- HW had an acceptable understanding of its IT needs when it decided to select SMS, but no single report or document contained a comprehensive analysis of HW needs
- best practice for purchasing IT, in terms of tendering and contracting, was not followed through the SMS purchase process
- the directors' involvement in the purchase was understandable given the discontinuity of management
- the decision to enter into the SMS contract was made too quickly. This had consequences for:
  - an inadequate contract, light on detail, and which was finalised before completion of an implementation study
  - finance for the purchase which had not been fully arranged when the contract was signed
  - failing to provide enough time for consultation with front-line clinical staff, the main users of the IT system
- the failure to carry out an implementation study before entering into the contract was a serious failure of process. This left inadequate time for management and external legal advisers to assess the functionality of SMS
- HW chair Jack Jenkins had no conflict of interest in the SMS deal.

The Bell Gully report implied several additional problems with the SMS process. As noted, these included that clinical views may not have been adequately canvassed or considered, that CCMAU and the health minister may have influenced board thinking, and that various reports comparing SMS and other options had been hastily prepared and considered. Bell Gully also highlighted the lack of continuity at all levels of decision-making, noting that when 'the board resolved to enter into contract with SMS, there were very few people from management who had been continuously involved in the project ... There was no continuous IT advice, whether internal or external, and external consultants had been used on a piecemeal basis' (Bell Gully 1999: 35).

Also in December 1999, merely a year after the SMS purchase, Simsion Bowles began delivering a series of reports and presentations to HW management and board members. These identified multiple problems with what they called the SMS 'infolinks project', leading to the ultimate recommendation that HW should discontinue implementation.

An initial draft report, dated 14 December, considered SMS 'functionality', probing two questions. First, would SMS meet HW's long-term information system needs? The answer was affirmative, provided that New Zealand modifications, questionable as noted, were implemented. Second, would SMS deliver better value over the existing Hospro system? Here it was suggested that the clinical support, patient accounting, and business executive view systems could deliver 'substantial value' with long-term investment. The Allegra suite, however, delivered 'no material benefit'. The report outlined five system architecture options for the way forward, from complete SMS implementation through to an SMS/Hospro combination (Simsion Bowles and Associates 1999).

A second report, delivered in February 2000, was a detailed consideration of strategic IT options. Four were provided, including deferring the project for six months while an IT strategy was developed, as well as discontinuing the infolinks project. Each option was costed and each, it was suggested, required negotiation with SMS. None guaranteed successful infolinks implementation (Simsion Bowles and Associates 2000a: 11). The report recommended HW develop an IT strategic plan and continue to implement only the SMS electronic clinical records and business executive view sub-projects at a cost of $17 million. The views of Chapman Tripp, who had assisted Simsion Bowles in their review, were provided in an appendix. While they agreed with the Simsion Bowles recommendation, their opinion was that '… the board must seriously consider termination/buy-out of the contract as a necessary option [as other options such as deferral may prove untenable]. The net result of advice HWL has received to date is that, while the SMS product itself is basically sound (at least in its vanilla form), HWL is not able to say this is the appropriate solution' (Simsion Bowles and Associates 2000a: 32).

Simsion Bowles' final report of April 2000 delivered a terminal blow to SMS. It recommended discontinuing the infolinks project as 'the option which is in the best interests of [HW]' (Simsion Bowles and Associates 2000b: 5). The rationale for this was clear:

> To continue would require major business process change in an environment where users are neither willing nor ready to participate. Significant additional funding is required to implement a system that would deliver, in our view, limited business value … discontinuing is potentially the cheapest option by a significant margin … There appear to be no tactical business imperatives that drive the implementation of the Infolinks project [no requirement nor desire for electronic medical records, uninterested business staff, and an organisation structure with limited ability to implement change and involve users effectively]. Further, a similar implementation project, with associated business process change, will probably be required in three to four years regardless of whether Infolinks proceeds or not (Simsion Bowles and Associates 2000b: 6).

A fundamental driver of the recommendation was the fact that SMS announced, in December 1999, that it would no longer be enhancing the Allegra suite of key technologies provided under the SMS contract. Maintenance support would be provided, but SMS would no longer be engaging in research and development of Allegra products. Instead, SMS recommended migrating, by 2003, to a new Novius product under development, requiring a further implementation project similar in size to SMS implementation. The implication was that HW would be responsible for funding future Allegra enhancements (Simsion Bowles and Associates 2000b: 14–15).

The cost of continuing with SMS was estimated at $25.2 million plus additional operating costs until 2007, when the SMS contract expired, of $10.9 million. This compared with an estimated total discontinuation cost of $16.3 million with additional capital costs of continuing to use Hospro until 2007 of $12.99 million. The cost of continuing with SMS was assessed as 'most likely [of all options] to vary from cost forecasts', therefore carrying higher financial risks (Simsion Bowles and Associates 2000b: 6, 12).

CCMAU commissioned an independent review, by consultants Seranova, of the Simsion Bowles project findings, also delivered in early April 2000 (Seranova 2000). This found that, for the main part, Simsion Bowles' had produced a thorough review of the HW situation, but that, in the absence of HW having an IT strategy or business case for SMS, their recommendations had been limited and largely based on cost comparisons. Seranova suggested that two further options were available to HW. One had been suggested by Simsion Bowles; the other involved using a web-browser interface to make the system more user-friendly. Both options were rejected by HW (Crown Company Monitoring Advisory Unit 2000; Health Waikato Ltd 2000).

At its 14 April 2000 meeting the HW board decided to terminate the SMS contract. CCMAU's advice to the Ministers of Health and of Finance was that the board's decision was 'reasonable' and 'based on sufficient information', and that Ministers should not intervene (Crown Company Monitoring Advisory Unit 2000: 4). On 2 May, the 'ditching' of SMS was announced (North 2000). Naturally, this was the subject of multiple media reports. Health Minister Annette King simultaneously declared that 'someone has to be held accountable', and asked four HW board members to resign because of their roles in the SMS purchase (King 2000). She also indicated that, had Jack Jenkins not previously stood down, she would have sought his resignation as well (New Zealand Press Association 2000c). Jenkins remained resolute, suggesting that 'the board took the decision on the information they had available' (New Zealand Press Association 2000b).

By the time SMS was terminated, the implementation of software and hardware was claimed to be around fifty percent complete, although not in a useable state. There were various reports of the total cost of the SMS fiasco. Generally, as noted in the introduction to this chapter, these were around $17 million. As Simsion Bowles suggested, the costs may have been much higher, with Annette King agreeing the total cost could be as high as $18 million (New Zealand Press Association 2000a). At least $9 million paid to SMS for software, licenses, and installation work was written off. In addition were the fees paid for the multitude of consultant reports, legal opinions, site visit costs, as well as management and staff time, the various staff resignations, and HW board director fees. Directors' fees in 1999 were approximately $270,000. The discontinuation meant that HW was left with its existing Hospro information system, which staff were accustomed to working with and required no reorganisation of work routines. In late 2005, Hospro remained in use. The HW experience ultimately added to the then Labour–Alliance coalition government's resolve that a health sector information technology strategy was required. As noted in Chapter 3 of this book, the WAVE project was launched in September 2000.

Conclusion

In the light of the events described in this chapter, the HW fiasco is remarkable for the fact that the SMS purchase ever occurred, given such uncertainty about the product at the time of purchase, plurality of opinion surrounding it, questions over clinical buy-in, and lack of an IT strategy on which to base purchasing decisions. Although reviews cleared all those involved in the SMS purchase of any wrongdoing, various factors appear to have contributed. These include preference for an off-the-shelf product already installed in another New Zealand location. Notably, HW management suggested SMS was 'proven'. Clearly, this was not the case and SMS installation at CCH had only just commenced at the time of the HW purchase. Also contributing was the apparent miscommunication of political preferences to the HW board in a context where hasty decision-making was required due to the impending need to ensure systems were Y2K compliant. Finally, the extent to which the combined sum of a multiple array of players and events worked to facilitate a fundamentally flawed decision cannot be discounted. Neither hard selling by SMS nor overzealousness by HW staff can be blamed for the decision. On the contrary, it appears that, buried in confusion, the board and staff failed to critically examine the bases for their thinking, while those who did disagree resigned from the organisation. It appears that incrementally and, finally, very hastily, weight turned in favour of SMS, perhaps due to the sense of urgency. It would be inaccurate to suggest SMS was favoured because the product was superior to alternatives, or that it was clearly the right one for HW.

The introduction to this chapter listed a series of lessons from the HW fiasco. To reiterate, the HW experience shows that:

• in public governance situations, with accountability shared between board and management, and with a 'bottom line' that includes adhering to government policy, it is very easy to preside over flawed decisions

- the solution to health care information system demands is more complex than may be provided for by off-the-shelf products, particularly where these are designed for use in other countries such as the United States
- a high level of health system and information system understanding is required for effective IT purchasing, along with detailed and carefully constructed strategic plans developed in concurrence with all implicated parties: clinical staff, management, and central government agencies
- it cannot be assumed that implementation of information systems will occur in a vacuum; indeed, implementation requires detailed planning, the purchase of systems designed for the purposes and contexts they are procured for, and considerable user commitment and organisational adaptation to new systems.

These themes are revisited in the concluding chapter.

5.

The INCIS Fiasco in the New Zealand Police Force

In early August 1999 the Integrated National Crime Investigation System (INCIS) was abandoned after almost ten years of work. INCIS was a highly ambitious development, based on then undeveloped technology, with a proposed 3125 personal computers linking all police stations to each other and to a national crime database. It would, it was claimed, improve criminal investigation and analysis for the Police. Efficiency gains, including less paperwork, would free up police for front-line duties, and lead to job savings. The completed system would find a ready overseas market. Projected financial benefits were huge.

The direct cost to the government of the INCIS fiasco, after an out-of-court settlement with IBM and the sale of computer hardware, was about NZ$100 million. This was out of an annual Police budget of around $800 million, creating a severe financial squeeze for Police. Additional indirect costs in terms of disruption, lost police time, hours spent 'fire-fighting' by other public officials and politicians, and opportunity costs, are virtually impossible to calculate. None of INCIS' major applications became operational. The Police were left with an organisation 're-engineered' around what was called a 'Community Policing Strategy', which itself was to be based around a functional INCIS system. There were a number of unsuccessful attempts to rescue the project, including a ministerial group that included senior ministers. The fiasco led to a report by a select committee of the New Zealand Parliament and a ministerial inquiry, followed by a review of IT monitoring regimes in the public sector. At its abandonment in 1999, INCIS was, and remains so far, the largest public sector computer failure in New Zealand's history.

The INCIS fiasco exhibited the traits of the typical failed ICT project, to the extent it could be seen as an 'exemplary failure'. This included:

- remarkably overblown expectations regarding ICT
- the attempted development of new and unproven technology
- management and reporting problems
- a naive faith in contracts to control development and seek redress when things went wrong
- lack of clarity on the aims and specifications of the system

- increasing the complexity of the project through specification changes and organisational restructuring.

As INCIS unfolded it showed many of the characteristics found in other computer failures such as:

- cultural and personality clashes
- massive cost and timeline overruns
- continual reassurances that things were going according to plan in the face of overwhelming evidence to the contrary.

Drawing on published accounts, government reports, archival material and interviews with contractors and government officials, this chapter examines and interprets the INCIS failure.

The Origins of the INCIS Project

INCIS has a long and convoluted history. In the twelve preceding years, a number of major Police information system developments (ISDs) had been attempted with limited success. As the Sapphire (1994) report documents, these included the Serious Investigation Crime Application (SICA), the National Information System (NIS), and the National Investigation of Crime Database (NICD). There were also two earlier versions of INCIS, the first of which was named the National Criminal Intelligence System. All these projects were largely failures, for reasons not entirely clear but which included a 'lack of support from the organisation' (Sapphire 1994: 5).[1] There was seen to be some benefit in 'prototyping requirements' and in evolution 'towards the solution detailed in the [later INCIS] Request for Proposal' through the NIS and NICD developments (Sapphire 1994: 5). These failures did not, however, discourage further projects, and the Police were keen to move away from the mainframe-based Law Enforcement System (LES), also known as the 'Wanganui Computer'. This was essentially a powerful record-keeping system that first went into operation in December 1976 and had grown incrementally since through various upgrades.

The origins of INCIS can possibly be traced back as far as the Project Serious Incident Computer Applications, which began in April 1985, but the final INCIS project began in earnest in the early 1990s. In November 1990, Azimuth Consulting examined a number of IS requirements for Police Systems. A Project Review on the previous INCIS project was carried out in November 1991 by Martyn Carr and David Cittandi, who had worked on its development. They argued that the previous INCIS focus had grown through time – an ironic observation given the later expansion of the INCIS project focused on here. The report recommended that the new project focus on the 'core business' of the Police rather than providing 'back room' intelligence. The report also noted that the previous INCIS project had failed to capture the support of the organisation, again highly ironic given that the final INCIS would result in strong front-line police resistance. A Price Waterhouse Report of 13 November 1991 made a number of suggestions on the concept of INCIS and this firm was then contracted to further develop the project.

Between December 1991 and March 1992, a scoping study was carried out to define the aims of the project. This study gained 'national support' from the Police. A workshop that included senior staff from police headquarters identified the 'key corporate strategies' that were to be supported by INCIS and the proposed boundaries of the project (Sapphire 1994). These were reviewed by representatives from different police regions, and some adjustments made.

During March and May 1992, a process called a 'business requirements definition' was carried out. Key requirements at the time included a proposed 'application data model', which defined the kinds of information INCIS would store and manipulate (e.g. locations of crimes); a model of the Police crime investigation process; and a statement of requirements for the proposed Crime Trend Analysis and Intelligence Analysis, whereby the INCIS system could provide statistics for and predictions about patterns of criminal offending. Other requirements included ease-of-use, training, and other support. These requirements were reviewed and approved by staff from headquarters and representatives from the regions (Sapphire 1994).

From May to October 1992, a feasibility study was carried out. This examined whether the INCIS requirements could be met and what the proposed benefits of the scheme were. Different types of software architecture[2] and storage and capacity requirements were examined, the latter by examining the use of the Wanganui Computer. Different proposals were costed and benefits calculated, based, it was claimed, on previous experience of systems elsewhere in the Police. As the Sapphire (1994) report noted:

> INCIS represented a significant investment opportunity for the Police and government but only if the entire system were to be deployed. In addition, the minimum cost of such a system was $67 million with a likely cost for a fully distributed system of around $85 million ($5 million less than the final tender price); in other words, the largest single capital investment by Police.

This proposal was presented to the Police National System Steering Committee on 10 September 1992 and, following their positive evaluation, the Police Executive Committee authorised the project team to proceed to tender. A change manager was appointed to the Project Team, as were a number of sworn personnel, with the object of developing a business case (Small 2000: 35).

From July to November 1992 the Project Team made known Police desires and requirements for the INCIS project to the wider marketplace. It noted that INCIS was unlikely to be achievable from off-the-shelf technology. Already the lofty ambitions for the project were becoming evident, with discussion of technology marketable around the world and the need for 'a world-class team to achieve this ambitious goal' (Sapphire 1994: 7).

A Request for Information was developed during late 1992. This outlined mandatory criteria for firms to address if they wished to be considered as the prime contractor. The Request for Information was issued in November 1992 and sent on request to 141 potential suppliers, with sixty-nine responses received and twenty organisations requesting to be considered as prime contractor (Small 2000; Sapphire 1994).[3] Of these, four were selected: Andersen Consulting, GCS/IBM, Marconi Speech and Information Systems, and McDonnell Douglas. Each was sent a Request for Tender, with ten volumes of supporting questions and documentation, which discussed the business 'vision' of the Police for INCIS, and examined the technology that would support that vision. However, no preferences for management or technology systems were outlined.[4] That ambitions were overreaching was further suggested as a result of Police visits to Australia, Canada, England, Jersey, and the United States of America during 1993. No similar systems were found in operation. As Crewdson noted:

> We really set the path back in the 1970s with the Wanganui computer system. We didn't put enough time or money into it to keep it up to scratch.

> When I was asked to look at whether we should enter into a new project, I looked at the then current Wanganui system [LES and NIS] and the rest of our computing services and it wasn't close to meeting our needs. Probably it met 30 to 40% of them.

> We went to the world to see if we could buy off the shelf. There was nothing there in 1994 and there's nothing there now that integrates everything (Jackson 1998).

Initially tenders were received from IBM, Andersen Consulting, and McConnell Douglas. Police were not happy with the initial tenders, and requested further additions. McConnell Douglas's response was not seen as adequate, and they were excluded from the process, a decision upheld by internal Police review processes in the face of a challenge to the decision by McConnell Douglas subcontractor, Eagle Technology. Questions regarding the tendering process were raised and investigated a number of times. Some requirements were considered unrealistic by the contractors. For example, all pictures were required to download to the client computers in less than ten seconds.

Both Andersen Consulting and IBM were asked to rebid, and their responses were analysed on the INCIS Project Tender Rebid Evaluation of 12 July 1993. This rebidding process was long and tortuous, with 1000 questions directed to IBM and 600 questions to Andersen Consulting. While problems were seen with both rebids, initial evaluations favoured IBM, because it was seen as 'more compliant' and 'closest to enabling the Police's vision to be achieved' (Sapphire 1994: 9).[5] During July and August 1993, discussions continued between IBM and the Police, and IBM were given written confirmation that they were the preferred supplier. Partly because of a wish to avoid legal problems with the term 'tender', between December 1993 and March 1994 the Request for Tender was reissued as a Request for Proposal, in eight volumes, finally delivered on 3 December 1993. This led to a complete rebid from IBM, which contained significant changes from earlier bids.

Problems continued with the Project Team as members left and new members were appointed. Questioning of the IBM proposal also continued, with 1500 different issues raised by the Project Team. Many of these were not addressed before the contract was finally signed, a point noted at length in subsequent evaluations. Crewdson was instrumental in smoothing over the difficult relationship. This degree of uncertainty regarding the project, and the blustering response of IBM to questions, were again strong warnings to the Police that INCIS may not have been achievable. As the Sapphire Report (1994: 10) noted:

> Whilst IBM conceded that most of the points raised were valid, IBM had become concerned that its team did not have time and knowledge to answer the questions raised, it believed that many of the points raised 'questioned' its solution and it felt that it shouldn't address these questions until after the contract was signed.

In parallel with the tender process, the INCIS business case was prepared by the Police, and was complete by 12 May 1993, with Tony Crewdson, the future project director, instrumental in its development. Refinements continued after this date, however. The business case was based on previous positive assessments of the project by the Project Team, as reviewed by other police officers, with cost initially estimated between $70 million and $100 million. The business case of 12 May 1993 saw the purpose of INCIS as supporting 'operational policing by providing improved crime-related information, investigation and analysis capabilities to help ... detect and apprehend offenders [and] reduce crime.' This would be achieved by providing:

- 'criminal information' on offences and 'subjects of interest' in those offences
- 'crime trend analysis' with tools to extract, analyze, present and disseminate crime-related information
- 'intelligence analysis' with tools to 'extract, analyze present and disseminate "soft" data from serious investigations'
- 'performance measurement'
- support for special operations and security groups.

Costs were expected to include capital expenditure of $88 million, development and implementation of $4.1 million, training of $10.4 million, and annual operating costs of $13.1 million. This gave a lifetime cost of $185.5 million, at what was then a net present value (NPV)[6] of $135.4 million (Small 2000). INCIS was expected to save 1.9 million police hours per year through 'reduced paperwork, flatter hierarchy and improved workflow'. This was expected to lead to savings of $74.1 million per annum. It was also expected that $14.2 million annually would be saved on the computer systems then in operation. Through savings to other departments, expected overseas sales of $45 million, increased safety for officers, improved crime prevention abilities, operational support and 'above all, improved relationships with the community through the above changes' INCIS was expected to generate $566.1 million in benefits. This was a NPV in 1993 of $336 million, providing an overall expected net benefit of over $200 million (Small 2000). These projected benefits, it would later emerge, verged on the delusional.

The business case and supporting documentation outlined a compelling vision of the remarkably powerful tool that INCIS was envisaged to be. INCIS would combine all Police databases and link them to all stations through a network of 3125 PCs. Visual images, indexes for text, documents, incidents reports, and so on would be stored in central host sites, able to be accessed from any part of New Zealand. Relevant electronic case files would likely be stored at particular stations where the information was first captured but would be able to be copied to other stations and work sites. Police would be able to enter their notes onto PCs and be directly interfaced with other aspects of the justice system. The proposed system included portability, as laptop computers could be taken into the field and files accessed from remote sites. Proposed 'speedbooks' (laptop computers with special software) would allow relevant files to be updated automatically as data was entered. Questions could be directly addressed to databases, including multiple stage questions so, for example, as to eliminate suspects by various characteristics such as crime history, location, identifying marks and so on. The system could be used to develop, and present in graphical form, crime statistics and trends. Included was a proposed 'geographical information system enabling information to be viewed spatially as points on a map; further refinement would enable information behind each of these points to be queried as the user "drilled down" into the map' (Small 2000: 237). Much of the technology promised did not exist and was never developed, and of the remarkable applications promised, INCIS finally delivered only a graphic user interface (similar to the graphic interfaces found on desktop PCs) to the Wanganui Computer, and an e-mail system.

The Police consulted with various government agencies, including the central agencies (Treasury, State Services Commission and the Department of the Prime Minister and Cabinet) and the Department of Justice, which 'believed that an integrated approach to the development of IT systems in the area of criminal justice if maximum efficiency benefits were to be obtained [was appropriate]' (Waitai 1999). Various ministers were also briefed. A 22 July 1993 review by consultants Ernst and Young – commissioned jointly by Treasury and Police to report on 'strategic considerations', the business case, and the preferred IBM bid – concluded that the INCIS case was 'based on a sound technical solution', was 'consistent with the corporate strategy of Police,' and that it had 'a well argued business case for an affirmative investment decision' (Ernst and Young 1993: 4). However the report raised a number of reservations, including the level of overseas development involved, the need for 'proof of technical viability and deliverability', and the need for the implementation plan to be completed before the completion of the contract negotiations (Ernst and Young 1993: 8). A number of these issues were still not addressed by the time the contract was finally signed. The Minister of Information Technology, Maurice Williamson, also noted a number of concerns with the 'INSYS' (sic) project in a meeting with the Police Commissioner, including the long-time viability of the planned IBM OS/2 operating system (IBM's Windows competitor) and the possible costs and delays of converting this to Windows NT, 'the grandiose' nature of the project and problems with training and support (Williamson 1993). Partly in response to Williamson's concerns and other concerns regarding the tendering process, KPMG were contracted by the Police to report on this process. On 31 January 1994, KPMG recommended continuing with OS/2 and reported that the procurement process had followed industry best practice (Small 2000: 40). This positive assessment of the procedure process was confirmed after an investigation by a QC appointed by the State Services Commission, at the request of the Minister of Information Technology. On 21 February 1994, Williamson wrote to the Minister of Police, John Luxton, and noted that 'Police have opted for a higher risk solution than that which might have been provided by an international standard solution.' But he concluded, based on the assurances given, that 'it would appear that the contractual obligations on the vendor are strong enough to minimise the risks involved' (Williamson 1994). This would prove, most emphatically, not to be the case.

When, after several months, an embargo that the government had placed on discussion of the project before the 1993 election ended, Peter Doone, then Deputy Commissioner and the 'Executive Sponsor' of INCIS, established a number of 'liaison officers'. These officers were to facilitate communications between the Project Team, the developers, and the front-line police who would be expected to use the systems. However, tension between front-line police on one hand, and police management, the INCIS project, and the related Community Policing Initiative on the other, became a continuing feature of the development.

Various papers were presented to Cabinet in March and April 1994. The Cabinet Strategy Committee, a key cabinet committee of the National government, recommended that INCIS proceed, and Cabinet granted approval on 24 April. Expected benefits from INCIS were now $380 million in efficiency gains, export sales of $45 million, and stationery savings of $7 million, as well as avoiding expenditure on the redevelopment of other systems at $30 million and savings on operating expenses of $55 million. This was a total benefit of $517 million over eight years or $303 million NPV in 1994 (at 10 per cent). The cost was now estimated to be $203 million over eight years (then a NPV of $140 million). This included capital expenditure of $97 million and operating expenditure of $105 million. The government was to contribute $62 million in capital contributions, while the Police would fund the rest within its existing budget. The efficiency gains were mainly to be delivered by savings of around 11 per cent of the hours worked by police personnel, with 30 per cent savings to be delivered to the Crown. These savings were mainly to be delivered by reducing sworn personnel by 540 by June 2000 (Waitai 1999). Even within the government, Police projections on INCIS were treated with some scepticism (Fisk 1993). KPMG advised again that the Police should continue with OS/2. On 31 August Price Waterhouse withdrew from the project, and the Project Manager Martyn Carr, now with Sapphire Technology Ltd, prepared a handover report, which noted a number of problems and risks with INCIS (Sapphire 1994). These were seen to be manageable by the Project Sponsor, Deputy Commissioner Peter Doone, and not 'grounds to review the position' (Small 2000: 42).

Contract negotiations with IBM continued through 1993 and 1994. These negotiations were led by Colin Jacobs, with Tony Crewdson and Martyn Carr representing the Police. On 19 August 1994, Peter Doone reached agreement with IBM that outstanding issues had been addressed and both parties shook hands. However, IBM raised several additional issues and there was further negotiation until the contract was finally signed on 14 September 1994, although a number of issues remained unresolved. The contract would prove to be insufficient to control the project.

The INCIS Project Begins

The INCIS Request for Proposal[7] and contract was over 4000 pages. The Police established another INCIS Project Team with Superintendent Tony Crewdson as Project Director in October 1994.[8] Crewdson was an experienced and well-regarded officer with some experience in IT, but not in managing large IT projects. It was not until October 1998 that a project manager with experience in managing large-scale ISDs was appointed. To manage the organisational change and restructuring that was to accompany INCIS, a Change Management Team was established, reporting directly to Deputy Commissioner of Resource Management (and later Commissioner) Peter Doone. Doone was initially the INCIS project sponsor, appointed in June 1993. Price Waterhouse was appointed to audit the INCIS project in December 1994. Originally INCIS was to have been jointly managed by 'Partnering Meetings' of IBM and the Police. In May 1995 these meetings were abandoned and replaced by an Executive Control Group to try to reduce the dependence on IBM.

The INCIS program was designed to be delivered in two sections. The first was to install PC networks in all police stations, thus replacing the Wanganui systems 'with new Suspect and Offence Information Systems, Crime Trend Analysis, Intelligence Analysis and Mail Facilities'. The second was to implement a 'Case and Investigation System' early in 1997 (Small 2000: 28). The two sections were later changed to Iterations One, Two, and Three (with Release One) and then to Increment One, Two, and Three. From the first, there were problems with the INCIS software architecture. The Sapphire Report (1994) expressed concern that IBM could not demonstrate how the 'process manager' would work, or how this software would be built, during the INCIS evaluation process. The process manager application was to co-ordinate the operation and integration of the various software components of INCIS, and so was central to the project. The process manager was never successfully developed.

Problems with the contract and time slippages were evident from the first. INCIS began with a supposedly complete specification in the Request for Proposal and contract. However, it became apparent in February/March 1995 that the contract specifications did not contain sufficient detail to begin the design. In response, between March and October 1995, operations Discovery 1 and 2 were carried out to create detailed specifications. The delivery of the first release of INCIS was scheduled for April 1995, and the second (with new INCIS applications) in the following July. But projected completion dates continually slipped. The 'INCIS Liaison Update Newsletter' of January 1995 gave the end of 1996 as a completion date for the first release, and early 1997 for the second implementation, but in January 1995 Cabinet papers proposed the first delivery would be delayed until March 1997, and the second until December. Costs were also blowing out. The INCIS Project Status Report of June 1995 noted the 'effort and resources required to complete … will be considerably larger than originally anticipated' (Crewdson 1995: 13). The October 1995 Price Waterhouse report reiterated concern about slippages in delivery dates.

Management problems soon became evident. The Police dithered over decisions. Personality conflicts erupted. The replacement of the 'partnering arrangement' for managing the project with the Executive Control Group in May 1995 was supported by the Police Director of IT (Greg Batchelor) but opposed by the INCIS Project Director (Tony Crewdson). Personality disputes between the two became particularly heated and Crewdson offered his resignation during 1995 (Waitai 1999). Batchelor even claimed that the project report of December 1996 was misleading, something denied by Doone (1999),[9] called into question Crewdson's competence, and regarded him as too closely tied to IBM (Waitai 1999). For his part, Batchelor was instrumental in pushing for specification changes that increased the complexity of the project. The relationship was particularly complicated; although Crewdson had been appointed 'Project Director' in October 1994, this was something of a misnomer and he reported to Batchelor, appointed as Director of IT in November 1994. Crewdson was not necessarily comfortable with this arrangement (Waitai 1999).

Technology changes were also signalled in the first year of the project, with the Police requesting changes to the wide area network, the local area network, and the desktop operating systems. In May 1996, the Police requested that the operating system of the INCIS 'client' computers (desktop and laptop) be changed from IBM's OS/2 to Microsoft Windows NT. A consultancy firm, Logica, assessed the changes and reported that *30 per cent* of the then current project requirements were outside the scope of the original specifications. The change of the client operating system required that the (Windows NT) desktop users log in to OS/2 servers, and this was a 'world first' development. Police were advised by IBM that an immediate move to Windows NT desktops logging in to an OS/2 server was not feasible with the technology available at the time. Nor was this decision to switch from OS/2 supported by Project Director Crewdson, but the Director of IT (Batchelor) and Maurice Williamson (the Minister of Information Technology) favoured it (Matthews 1996). In July 1996, IBM advised the Police that guarantees of the performance and response time were to be waived because of the change to Windows NT and the network. The Police, however, pressed ahead, and agreement was reached on 14 October 1997. IBM absorbed an additional $10 million for the cost of the changeover, while the Police contributed $1.5 million. The Police also pushed for a change from the Token Ring local area network to Ethernet, despite two evaluations supporting the Token Ring. After negotiation, 'customer preference' was the reason given by the Police for the changes. The wide area network was also changed – avoiding the usual change process and without competitive tendering (Waitai 1999). Implementation faced considerable problems. To give one example, NZ Telecom provided the Police with a computer application which would display the phone numbers of houses close to a specified address. IBM agreed to take over this application, and the Telecom service was discontinued. It was subsequently found that the IBM application was two to three times slower than Telecom's application.

In March 1996, Price Waterhouse outlined concerns about completing the project on time and on budget, and noted problems with decisions still to be made on the project architecture. In its June report, this same firm described the INCIS project as high risk and in subsequent reports 'very high'. To the last, however, Police reports continued to reassure the government that the project was achievable. Indeed, some reports were almost upbeat, despite the continuing problems. In a December 1996 response to the Price Waterhouse report, Crewdson noted that the Police and IBM project management saw the project as high risk, and noted that delays in the provision of information from IBM had heightened this perception, but still regarded the 'potential cost exposure' as manageable with IBM 'willing to make substantial concessions'. Crewdson also noted that the establishment of a Project Steering Committee and the recruitment of 'highly skilled' technicians and management would ensure adequate control (Crewdson 1996). As one contractor noted in an interview with the authors, project reports were 'wonderful works of fiction' and auditing was 'a joke'.

By early 1997 monitoring agencies were aware the project was facing difficulties. In February, Treasury was already voicing concern about the reporting on INCIS, noting the non-production of the September 1996 INCIS report (Treasury 1997). Meanwhile the State Services Commission noted 'whispers' about the state of the INCIS project, including that it was 'at least 6 months behind schedule' and that the 'Police's current funding proposals [included] a request for reinstatement of $10 million a year which represents much of the promised INCIS savings' (Rapley 1997). In March 1997, the Secretary for the Treasury wrote to the Treasurer and the Minister of Finance noting that INCIS was 'behind schedule by 9 months' and 'forecast to cost $104 million, rather than the original budget of $97 million' with the 'potential for additional cost overruns' (Treasury, 1997).

In response to such concerns, a joint review was commissioned by Treasury and Police, to be conducted by Andersen Consulting. Andersen reported in May 1997 that around $55 million of the $95 million budget had been expended or incurred, with projected cost overruns of $8 million. This firm also reported that the project was eight to twelve months behind schedule. While Andersen noted there was 'considerable risk' associated with the project, it recommended continuation and that Police better manage the project and contract. Treasury were aware that the situation was even more serious than Andersen allowed, noting in June that the cost overruns of INCIS could be $20–50 million, and discussing the possibility of project termination.

This time, the response was to establish an Executive Control Group, consisting of the Deputy Commissioner of Police, the Police Director of Information and Technology, the Police INCIS Project Director, the Managing Director of IBM (NZ), the Solutions Integration Manager (IBM Asia Pacific), and Project Manager (IBM NZ). The group was to meet fortnightly to monitor and review the project. In early 1997 the then Director of Police IT, Greg Batchelor, resigned.[10] Communication between IBM and the Police was an ongoing problem throughout the project, and the relationship between the Police and IT contractors was often strained. In June 1997 the INCIS Project Internal Audit noted the continual 'deterioration in the relationship between IBM and Police', the 'lack of access to IBM personnel', and the inability or unwillingness of IBM to respond to questions in writing (Price Waterhouse 1997: 2). This tension exhibited signs of culture clash – the hierarchical Police culture, where often-domineering police expected their orders to be followed and where authority was often valued above expertise, grated considerably on contractors.

In September 1997 a fundamental change was made to the software system architecture. As one contractor put it, the INCIS team 'biffed it' and started again. The software architecture of INCIS was changed to a traditional software environment similar to the old-fashioned 'Wanganui Computer'.[11] This required substantial re-specification and rewriting of the system. A further systems analysis,

Operation Obstat, was carried out from 18 September to 31 November 1997 to re-specify what was required to complete the INCIS contract, and on 5 December 1997, Police and IBM signed a deed of variation of contract. The variation involved the commitment of a further $20 million for more development work. IBM threatened to withdraw unless the amount was forthcoming. This sum was contracted for by the Police without the required authority from Cabinet. Treasury only became aware of the contractual variation from the press. Cabinet moved to accommodate the unauthorised expenditure, but directed that the Police Commissioner's delegated spending authority be reviewed (Waitai 1999). The Ministers of Finance and Police, and the Associate Treasurer, directed that an independent external review of Police administrative and management levels and structures be carried out 'in order to identify opportunities for achieving efficiency [financial] savings' (Minister of Finance *et al*. 1998).

In October 1997 rumours were circulating in the Police and outside the government that delays in the INCIS project were due to 'costly cockups' (Chamberlain 1997: 43). Even though the entire INCIS project was being rewritten and was already a year late, reassurances continued. Project Director Tony Crewdson, in an interview with the magazine *North & South,* noted that the 'reality is we can't prove [the benefits of INCIS] until the thing is up and running. We are not dazzled by technology. It's only a tool. Used wisely, tools can provide a lot of relief.' But he maintained his enthusiasm for the project, describing it as a 'big Internet', phasing out paperwork altogether, with Police able to access a 'one stop data entry' through laptops in their cars. Information gathering and data analysis would allow Police to look at patterns of crime, while 'Crime mapping will … permit police to predict where problems are likely to crop up and plan combat strategies' (Chamberlain 1997: 43). However, the same article reported 'police of all ranks are sneeringly cynical at the notion that being able to take a laptop in the squad car will compensate for fewer staff' (Chamberlain 1997: 43).

From December 1997 to August 1998, IBM delivered more than 3000 workstations and associated hardware to the Police. This represented a significant proportion of the value of the contract to IBM. The cost of infrastructure was supplied largely at full cost by IBM. As subsequent evaluations of INCIS pointed out, having the developer of the project also supply the hardware creates a conflict of interest and it is generally recommended that hardware supply and project development be kept separate. (At least a substantial discount for such a large purchase might have been expected.) Each police station using INCIS was to be supplied with a considerable array of equipment, including a PC, a printer, network router, and so on. Almost no INCIS applications were available and, with the system not in operation, many laptops sat unused in a warehouse near Auckland airport for a considerable time, at risk of becoming obsolete. Indeed, some required upgrading as they lacked sufficient memory to run the operating system. Furthermore, in an interview with the authors, one contractor noted the difficulty in even locating the stored equipment.

In May 1998 Cabinet approved a further $1 million to strengthen the project management. An external expert was recruited as INCIS project manager in October 1998 and a KPMG Peat Marwick partner was appointed to the INCIS Executive Control Group. There was also pressure on Crewdson to resign, the State Services Commission noting that 'the incumbent project director has been off-site since May and Police are negotiating with him about his future employment within or outside of Police' (Provost 1998). This bald statement downplays the degree of tension over Crewdson's employment and the management of the project, which was noted in June to be one of 'high drama' with legal ramifications for the Police, and with Crewdson seen as a threat to the project. Crewdson left the INCIS project in May 1998 and the Police in October 1998, to be replaced by Stewart Watson. Before his appointment, Watson was assured INCIS was largely under control. Once in the job, he found there were two 'different' projects: on one side IBM, and on the other, the Police. Watson also noted that a considerable bureaucracy existed to manage the contractual relationship, and that the relationship between the two was difficult (Small 2000: 163). The large number of overseas-based IBM employees working on the project further compounded difficulties.

In May 1998, in the face of continuing questions about INCIS, an Ad Hoc Official Committee for IT Monitoring was established, chaired by the Deputy State Services Commissioner. The Police were required to report monthly to this committee. In June, Andersen Consulting presented a report examining the extent to which the Police had complied with the previous report of May 1997. As Treasury noted, the revised contract 'did not include end to end performance guarantees ...', the Police did not explore options to the project, and the project timetable had 'no allowance for delays nor was a specific amount of money set aside for cost overruns as is normally the case with large projects' (Shennan 1999).

To allay their concerns, Treasurer Winston Peters and the Secretary to the Treasury visited senior IBM executives in New York. Assurances were given that the project would be completed, although no timeframe was given, and IBM made available additional staff to work on it. A law firm, Philip Fox, was engaged by the Police and Treasury to undertake a review of the varied contract, in the wake of the extra unauthorised $20.17 million allocated. Then, in February 1999, the Police notified other government officials that further delays were expected. The progress of Increments one and two was reviewed, and it was found, rather bizarrely, 'that increment 1 was being managed in accordance with the best practice project management techniques' (emphasis added) (Waitai 1999). Police also received a detailed project plan from IBM for Increment two. Equally bizarre, the 'INCIS Increment Two Project Scope Review' stated in April that 'Police appeared to have managed this project extremely well, to the point of calling it 'perfect project management' and that 'Police [had] demonstrated [a] rigorous approach to managing the scope of INCIS (emphasis added)'. However termination of the project was already being considered in a Police letter to the State Services Commission, which listed implications for the cancellation of INCIS, including legal liability to IBM for up to the full value of the contract ($94 million) less funds paid to date ($67 million), and releasing IBM from liability for $30 million in extra application development costs (Matthews 1998).

Meanwhile, reassurances continued. On 11 January 1999, the Ad Hoc Committee on IT claimed 'mechanisms have been put in place to facilitate effective management of the identified risks' and estimated the cost to complete the INCIS project at $119 million (Matthews 1999: 5–6). Another report in early 1999 by the Gibraltar Group estimated the cost to complete INCIS would now be in the region of capital costs of $156 million and operating costs rising to $70 million in 2000/1, with a likely extension of twelve months over its expected June 1999 completion (Soar 1999). When the expected completion date moved out to May 2000 for Increment one and November 2000 for Increment two, Treasury became aware that the slippages, which they blamed on IBM, were getting out of control. Although continuation of the project was canvassed, abandonment was also being openly considered. Because of the delays of INCIS, the LES Police IT system (i.e. the Wanganui Computer) also required alterations to fix the 'Y2K bug' so it would run after the year 2000. State Services Commission personnel, now closely involved with the governance of INCIS, had formed the opinion that IBM could not 'deliver the goods' for the INCIS contract. They decided the best option was to halt the project and negotiate a graceful exit. In May, Treasurer Bill Birch notified Cabinet that IBM had informally advised officials 'that it does not intend to complete Increment Two of INCIS due to the time and cost of completion' (Birch 1999: 1). Investigations were then made into two alternatives to INCIS: PULSE, used by the Irish police, and VersaTerm, used by the Royal Canadian Mounted Police.

In June 1999, a Ministerial Group was established with a brief to review and monitor the project. This included front-bench senior ministers including the powerful 'minister for everything', Treasurer Bill Birch, and Minister of Finance Bill English, as well as the Ministers of Commerce, Police, and Associate Minister of State Services. The chief executives of the Treasury, State Services Commission and the Department of the Prime Minister and Cabinet, and the Police Commissioner, were required to oversee INCIS and report to the ministerial group. There was intense media interest in INCIS at this stage, but statements from the government and the Police continued to indicate it would continue. The Police Association chairman, Greg O'Conner, noted INCIS had 'not impacted on any police officers' lives' and 'so far, it's only being used by the intelligence people' (Bell 1999: 24). The Justice and Law Reform Select Committee of the New Zealand Parliament was also becoming increasingly concerned and requested that the Audit Office review the project – a request Audit was unable to fulfil in totality as some issues were *sub judice* (Waitai 1999).

Conclusion: The Death of INCIS

IBM's first threats to withdraw came in late 1997, and discussions about termination within the government go back at least as far. As the Treasurer noted in May 1999, IBM informally advised officials that it did not intend to complete Increment two, and the government began canvassing its options in response (Birch 1999). However, the INCIS project officially ended in early August 1999 when IBM advised the Police that it would not continue this work without renegotiating the contract to include further payment. The public response of the Police and government was that IBM should continue work under the existing conditions and terms of payment. IBM repudiated the contract on 17 August and insisted 'the goalposts have been moving since day one' and that it was owed 'a substantial amount of money' (Brown 1999:1).

On 17 August 1999, the Attorney-General filed proceedings against IBM in the High Court at Wellington. The Crown sought judgement in relation to three causes of action and sought various forms of relief, including two sums over $3 million (excluding GST). A Statement of Defence and Counterclaim was then filed by IBM seeking $75 million and court costs in compensation for losses it claimed it sustained from the project. IBM maintained from Tokyo that they had 'met their contractual obligations [and] have done more than required. We are very proud of what we have already delivered which has resulted in a modernisation of police computer services' (Beynen 1999: 1). One hundred and twenty-five contractors working on the project were made redundant, while of the 25 IBM employees, between '10 and 20' were to stay on as 'part of the company's maintenance obligations [with] the rest "reassigned" within IBM' (Beynen 1999: 1). Subsequently, the government and IBM settled out of court. IBM paid the Crown $NZ25 million, while the Crown paid IBM $NZ18 million for work already completed (*Evening Post* 1999). The mainframe was sold at a reported price of $1 million, knocked down from the original cost of $7.6 million. Doone took early retirement when he was accused of trying to unduly influence a junior police officer when Doone's partner was stopped in a random breath-testing incident. Deputy Commissioner Barry Matthews left to take up a senior post in Western Australia (*Press* 2000). The Police continued using the Wanganui Computer.

An initial Commission of Inquiry was abandoned in favour of a Ministerial Inquiry, headed by Dr Francis Small, which reported to the Minister of Justice in the newly elected Labour government on 19 October 2000. The recommendations of the Small Inquiry were:

- business cases should reflect overall technology resources and risks as well as financial issues
- projects should use proven technology. If not, there should be 'increased risk management' processes

- projects need adequate skilled and experienced management
- there should be separate contracts for infrastructure and applications
- independent quality assurance should be used
- contracts should only be signed when all relevant issues have been resolved
- procedures for Cabinet approval need to be tightened to assure Cabinet receives adequate information and an appreciation of the risks of the project.

In April 2001, the government indicated that it would accept all these recommendations, which were reflected in subsequent monitoring regimes (see Chapter 7) (Mallard 2000).

In the wake of the INCIS failure, Police needed substantial additional funding to pay for the project, including $94.6 million during 2000. This included a $66 million write-down for computer hardware, software, and network costs associated with the project. Countless police hours were wasted on INCIS and considerable disruption was caused, while a large number of other officials and politicians also found themselves drawn into the disaster. The drain on Police budgets led to buildings not being maintained and fleets of cars not being upgraded during 1996–8 (Hawkins 2001a; Hawkins 2001b). The police force was restructured around a computer system that never became operational. In the end, INCIS provided little more than a number of 'smart' terminals to the Wanganui Computer and an e-mail system.

In 2000 UNISYS replaced OS/2 with Windows NT on police servers. In April 2001, Police began planning an organisation-wide computer system, quickly dubbed 'INCIS 2' by the media (Pamatatau 2001). The Police now claimed to reject large scale IS projects, claiming developments should be 'incremental, evolutionary and modular, acknowledging that there is no 'silver bullet' solution for Police IT requirements' (Police 2001: 6). In 2002, a contract was signed with UNISYS to supply and manage police systems. There was a gradual upgrade of computer systems and a phased removal from the Wanganui Computer to a new National Information Application intended to be the main information system for the Police, with the system being developed in-house in conjunction with IBM (NZ Police 2004). This was completed in June 2005. In May 2005 it was announced the Wanganui Computer would be decommissioned. In June 2005, the Wanganui Computer was finally switched off, after almost thirty years of successful and faithful service.

6.

Landonline: Qualified success or partial failure?

Landonline is an electronic database of land title and survey information held by Land Information New Zealand. Land Information New Zealand (LINZ) is the government agency responsible for managing New Zealand's title and survey information, with an archive of around 30 million records, including historical records going back over a century. Once the appropriate fees are paid, and the relevant software downloaded, users can search the Landonline database online for survey and title information. This is a highly sophisticated system, allowing users to search by various key words and call up detailed title documents, scanned images of original titles, and graphical survey plans. Surveyors can prepare and lodge survey documents and transactions without recourse to paperwork. Lawyers and others can lodge title documents and title transactions electronically. Electronic title transactions are instantaneous. As proof of identity, users require 'digital certificates', for which they need to pay a fee.

Despite the sometimes excited rhetoric, Landonline had the reasonably modest aim of converting manual processes to electronic ones. Technical challenges were evident in combining different existing technology and data, rather than always building them from scratch. As the LINZ's chief executive noted in 1997:

> The technology for automating the survey system is not a world first. The world first aspect is the structuring of the data and pulling all the components together. The risk was that the survey and title data could not be integrated (Ballard 1997).

Nor was the development of the system seen as an opportunity to correct any perceived problems with the manual systems – existing records, that were possibly faulty, were not corrected. There were also no attempts to fundamentally reorder what were usual business practices, although this was a somewhat unintended outcome. The development of Landonline, in contrast to INCIS, had a presumption towards existing technologies and hardware.[1] The project was divided into contestable contracts, with financial penalties for non-delivery and time overruns built into contracts after its 'relaunch' in 1999.

Landonline was initiated in 1996, approved in 1997, and finally completed in

November 2003. During the lifetime of the development, it met with considerable difficulties, including timetable overruns of two or more years, and overruns from the initial budget of over 50 per cent. At one stage, Terralink, a government-owned enterprise contracted to develop some of Landonline's applications, went into receivership and was later sold to private owners. In 1999, Treasury recommended that the project be abandoned, and the government maintained a considerable degree of scepticism towards it. Monitoring mechanisms were tightened during the life of the project, particularly after it was relaunched in 1999. The development created some political excitement, and at times comparisons were made to the INCIS fiasco by the Labour and then the National opposition. Initial projections of the net present value (NPV) of the project turned out to be highly optimistic, and its financial benefits are still uncertain. Concerns continue regarding access to some historical documents. However, while many users are still reluctant to use some of its more sophisticated transactional functions, Landonline is considered a success by LINZ, and a qualified success by other evaluations. This chapter draws on files held at LINZ, as well as other archives, newspaper and magazine accounts, and a ten-page written response by LINZ to a series of questions. LINZ also commented on a draft of this chapter.

Initiation of Landonline
The aim of Landonline, according to LINZ, was to:

> develop an integrated secure national land title and survey system available from remote locations, and shorten transaction processing turnaround times down to 24 hours for 90% of transactions. The benefits of Landonline were considered to be lower processing fees charged by LINZ; lower professional fees charged by surveyors and conveyancers; and reduced interest payments charged by banks to people buying, selling, and developing property (LINZ 2004).

Discussion of the automation of titles and survey processes goes back to before the time that LINZ was established from the amalgamation of the Department of Survey and Land Information and the Land Titles Office in July 1996,[2] and the Landonline development drew on two existing processes. The first was the Digital Cadastral Database which gave an electronic index to spatial plans and was made available in mid-1996. The second was a text-based online database for titles. The electronic index of titles was made available to clients in early 1996 but had only limited searching options. In June 1996, Cabinet directed LINZ and Treasury to further consider options regarding the automation of future LINZ processes, and the cost and benefits of this, and to report to the Cabinet State Sector Committee by 28 February 1997. Capital funding of $13.662 million in 1997/8 and operational funding of $2.205 million were set aside by the government. A report by Price

Waterhouse Urwick in February 1997 estimated cost-savings benefits of automation to lawyers and surveyors would be $28.2 million per annum (Price Waterhouse Urwick 1997). This projection was found to be generally sound by the New Zealand Institute of Economic Research (Yeabsley 1997).

A business case was completed in early 1997 and expenditure of $95 million was projected over the life of the project. Various proposals for automation were evaluated, drawing on experiences in Australia, Canada, Hong Kong, South Korea, and Malaysia and considering 'output costs, internal and external benefits, net present value, risks and resource implications' (Office of the Minister of Lands 1997: 4). Expected benefits from the development were not overwhelming. Of the automation options considered, when compared to then current manual processes, none had a positive NPV when taking into account internal savings alone. Savings to LINZ from reductions in staff numbers and building costs did not offset the capital and operating costs of the system. However, NPV was positive when expected external benefits that would accrue to lawyers and surveyors and their clients were added to the equation. Further, as noted,

> the reduction in LINZ processing times resulting from automation will provide benefits to parties such as property developers, by reducing the need for bridging finance, for example. This benefit has not been quantified because of the difficulty in establishing when and to what extent it will be a real gain. The extent of the gain will differ for individual projects and will range from zero to positive benefits (Office of the Minister of Lands 1997: 5).

NVPs varied depending on the measure used, but, based on savings in wage costs, it was expected to be $33.4 million. Other expected gains included 'longer-term dynamic savings from users as they adjust … to the new, simpler automated system' (Office of the Minister of Lands 1997: 5). At the most optimistic, NPV was estimated at $100.4 million. Despite Treasury scepticism, this optimistic figure was used in projections. So-called 'external stakeholders' – that is, surveyors, solicitors, and so on – were projected to save $26 million annually. Staff would be reduced by 242, and seven regional LINZ offices would be closed. The preferred option – a full automation of LINZ's business – was finally approved by Cabinet in November 1997.

Readily available technology was to be used in the development. As the business case noted:

> access to the proposed system would be by common distribution architectures such as Internet, which enables use of cheap, commonly used browser software for both internal and external users. Customers would be able to complete land transactions from remote locations. The computer hardware … would conform to open standards,

thereby maximising the commercial advantages from contestable sourcing of hardware systems and software products. The proposed solution, encompassing hardware, software and data based technologies would avoid using leading edge technology. A robust demonstration and evaluation and permit system similar to LINZ's requirements would be required (Office of the Minister of Lands 1997: 7).

LINZ established a steering committee, chaired by the LINZ chief executive officer, which included 'key' internal and external shareholders. Its function was to oversee the separate stages of the development. The committee met monthly. The LINZ programme manager, who controlled finances, met weekly with the project managers. Projects required weekly written reports. Regular independent quality assurance was undertaken by the consultant Opticon. Consultation of 'stakeholders', both within and outside LINZ, was also undertaken. In November 1997, Cabinet decided that, every six months, LINZ must report on progress towards agreed milestones and on any commitments over $4 million to a subcommittee consisting of the Minister of Lands, the Minister Finance, and the Minister of Communications.

With the project approved, in an internal memo the LINZ chief executive commented:

> The programme will move ahead with building the computer systems from January 1998 and finish in 2001 with fully automated survey and titles processes.
>
> Our goal is secure national land title in survey system available from remote locations with a turnaround time of 24 hours for 90% of survey and title transactions (Ballard 1997).

The Project Begins

The Landonline contracts were characterised by the division of the project into different components (such as 'design', 'build' and 'implementation'), reflecting the new procurement regimes then being developed in the public sector. These were tendered separately. Management of the computer facilities was also tendered separately. After the project was revised and relaunched in 1999, contracts themselves were broken down into 'milestones' with payment contingent on completing each milestone and with penalty payments for delays. (Continual delays activated these penalty payments, which ran into the millions of dollars.) The project also required amendments to the Land Transfers Act 1952 and the Survey Act 1956.

The Landonline project was divided into two stages: Core Records System (Phase One or CR1) and Core Records System 2 (Phase Two or CR2). The contracts in both phases are summarised in Table 6.1.

Phase One

The first phase of the project involved the conversion of five million title records, over 1.2 million survey documents, and 1.3 million parcels into digital form. After

---

Phase One
- 1997 Design of the Core Record System (CRS) (PricewaterhouseCoopers)
- 1998 Construction of CRS (PricewaterhouseCoopers)
- 1999 Data conversion – convert all live and cancelled certificates of title and approximately 70% of surveyed land parcels into electronic form and upload these into the CRS database (EDS)
- 1999 Facilities management – purchase and support the hardware (EDS)

Phase Two
- 1999 Stage two feasibility study (PricewaterhouseCoopers)
- 2000 Stage two user requirements (Andersen Consulting)
- 2001 Construction of the stage two system (PricewaterhouseCoopers)
- 2002 Software maintenance (PricewaterhouseCoopers)

Table 6.1. Contracts in the Landonline Project
Source: LINZ (2004).

a PricewaterhouseCoopers (PwC) report in 1997, a range of systems was selected for the project. Phase One was started by LINZ, which funded a $2.8 million design phase completed by PwC in December 1997. LINZ and PwC signed an agreement on 30 September 1998 for the 'build and implementation' of Phase One and for the 'image project plan'. PwC was to develop the core record system application software, develop design specifications for the operating environment of the software, as well as provide a number of other services. This part of the contract was valued at approximately $11.225 million. The 'image plans project' involved the conversion of LINZ documents to digital format, and was valued at $3.4 million. Further services – 'the implementation services' – were provided to assist LINZ in the implementation project and had a value of approximately $1.8 million. Penalty payments would be made for delays. LINZ was able to terminate the project on the basis that it reimburse any PwC loss 'actually or reasonably' incurred. PwC's liability was limited to a maximum $15.7 million. LINZ's liability was limited to $1 million (Buddle Finlay 1999). As it would turn out, while PwC developed the design for Phase One, when awarded the build phase, they claimed the design could not be built. LINZ's $11.2 million contract with PwC would eventually run $10 million over budget, with cost overruns shared equally between PwC and LINZ.

Once the call for expression of interest was made for other contracts for Phase One, of the seventeen companies that registered interest, four were invited to tender. EDS was selected as the preferred supplier in late 1998 with a round of negotiations extending into mid-1999 before the contract was finally signed in June. Before LINZ tender documents were issued, Landonline programme manager Terry Jackson and two other officials visited Ontario in early 1998 to examine the

EDS project to automate Canadian land titles processes. However, this visit did not comprise part of the evaluation of the actual bids and other sites in Australia and elsewhere were also visited (Dominion 1999a). The awarding of the fixed price $102 million contract to EDS, which included scanning land titles and developing survey data ($49.4 million) as well as providing a facilities management service ($52.8 million), and which had originally been tendered as separate contracts before being rolled into one, led to a number of complaints from unsuccessful tenderers. Others were somewhat surprised at the cost of the facilities management contract awarded to EDS. Datamail, a subsidiary of New Zealand Post, along with another tenderer, discussed filing a formal complaint over the tendering process. Another tenderer filed Official Information requests regarding the process. One concern was that parcelling different tenders into one package gave EDS the ability to cross-subsidise work between different jobs. LINZ's response was that the tenders were let separately and awarded on their own merits. Providers were given the option to indicate savings if successful in more than one tender. These three tenders were only 'rolled into one' after detailed contract negotiations and after EDS had already been selected as the preferred supplier. It was claimed that EDS would deliver by avoiding duplication of work (*Dominion* 1999a).

In March 1999, EDS completed Y2K remediation work on LINZ's mainframe-based land-title system that was due to be phased out in the upgrade. In mid-1999, LINZ announced that Landonline would be accessible only through Windows.

Problems with Phase One – Termination Considered

Difficulties arose almost from the first. Initial costs and completion timeframes proved to be considerably optimistic. The LINZ annual report of 1998 noted:

> Landonline is a four-year project with a fixed budget and no contingency allowance. We will be 'lucky' to come in on time and budget while retaining expected functionality. Pressures are already showing.

> The automation program has been kept on budget to date by maximising the use of internal resources. This can only be sustained with declining demand for output activities and a willingness of funders to continue existing resourcing of these output activities. A change in either of these circumstances will cause difficulties (*Dominion*, 1999b).

In late 1998, LINZ reported the 'build and implement' project and the cost of the facilities management contract had increased beyond the amounts approved – by $6.7 million and $10.8 million respectively. The bids received for the conversion project were $19.5 million over the $55.6 million budgeted for (Ballard 1999: 3). In February 1999, the projected cost increased by $45.3 million to $140.3 million

(CSSECGA 1999). Projected completion dates moved out by 18 months. The delay was seen by LINZ chief executive Russ Ballard as 'due to design modifications to the system' (*Evening Post* 1999: 1), or 'the redesign of some software modules ... [with] more work involved in building some subsystems ...' (Pullar-Strecker 1999a: 2) and later to 'software glitches' (*Dominion* 1999b).

Termination was now considered. On 17 February 1999 the ministerial subcommittee directed LINZ to examine project termination, and requested an assessment by Treasury and the State Services Commission. An assessment gave qualified approval to the designs of the contract for PwC and the proposed contract with EDS (Buddle Finlay 1999). The build and implement project was continued with an increase in the contract price of $1.5 million for PwC to continue the project to 10 May 1999. A further payment of $0.4 million was made to that firm in May 1999.

By late May 1999, Treasury was advocating the abandonment of the project citing cost overruns, benefits deferred far into the future (twelve years), size and expense, and the small return for the size of the investment. The cost of terminating the project was estimated to be $15.3 million (including $9.2 million to buy out the PwC contract), with another $3.3 million required to replace obsolescent items, for document storage and disaster recovery. An Innovus Report of late May supported continuing the project, but argued the completion timeframe was too tight. The State Services Commission, while recognising Landonline was a 'very marginal proposition', also supported continuing the project, but with strengthened management and accountability mechanisms. LINZ insisted the project was viable and that it be continued. The external quality assurance consultants, Opticon, took umbrage at the negative tone (and accuracy) of some of the reports and also supported the continuation of the project. In addition, professional associations voiced support for the project. In June, the Primary Production Select Committee expressed concerns, and the Labour opposition began making Landonline, as well as INCIS, an issue of much controversy

Cabinet decided to continue, and essentially relaunch, the project on 14 June, on the proviso that its management be improved (Cabinet 1999). A budget of between $144 .4 million and $154 .1 million was approved. Funds were appropriated at $148.6 million. The NPV of the project had fallen dramatically from the initial $100.4 million, and was now expected to be between zero and $80 million, with $36.6 million being LINZ's best estimate. However, NPV values were calculated on the very high take-up rates of the new system by conveyancing firms (at the 95 per cent level) and surveying firms (at the 85 per cent level). In addition, LINZ did not take into account marginal cost that might accrue to service as they converted to the new Landonline system, such as PC upgrades (Mallard 2000). These projections would prove to be highly optimistic and user resistance to the system continued well after it was completed.

Cabinet finally approved the fixed-price EDS contract of $52.8 million for data conversion and $49.4 million for facilities management services on 14 June, after the initial date of contract signing had been moved out from 10 May due to uncertainty over the continuance of the project. The facilities management contract was to run to March 2005. Before the contract was signed, EDS had already begun work, and 1.4 million survey plans had also already been imaged. The revised completion date was expanded outwards with March 2000 'the earliest that might be expected' for the completion of CR1; however, 'a more likely date is May 2000 and it could extend as far as September 2000, although the *likelihood of such an extreme overrun is remote* [emphasis added] (Luxton 1999: 11). This would again prove to be considerably optimistic.

In October 1999, it was claimed the software needed to implement Phase One was 'basically complete' and that a three months' testing programme would begin in November, with implementation starting in Dunedin in March 2000. EDS claimed to be working 'flat out' to develop software to convert the five million documents to be loaded on Landonline's database (Pullar-Strecker 1999b). In January 2000, LINZ estimated costs could be as high as $164 million.

In March 2000 the cost for the two-phase project was again estimated to be 'at least' $141.5 million. The LINZ chief executive, Russ Ballard, now blamed the blow-out on forecasting difficulties. These, he noted, were partly due to LINZ only having 'out of date overseas experience to look at and budgeting rules [that] required ... and the cheapest option be submitted.' As he noted:

> even where we had identified that there were potential [problems], those were not to be budgeted for. So the vast majority of the difference in budget is a forecasting problem, as opposed to our difficulties running a project (*Dominion* 2000c: 2).

While the chief executive was confident that the project would not now exceed this budget, he also noted it was unrealistic to expect it would not exceed $141.5 million (*Dominion* 2000c: 2).

By March 2000, EDS demonstrated they could meet the quality criteria for converted title data (Ballard 2000a). A number of minor problems were discovered in testing, but these were not expected to have any impact on implementation.

Implementation of Phase One

The implementation of Phase One was to be carried out over two years, beginning in March 2000 in Dunedin and Southland. Initial delays meant it began in April. Conversion of title records to digital form began on 3 April and other aspects began a week later. Problems and delays with conversions of titles and surveys to digital form as well as processing delays were ongoing. The initial completion date for conversion of title data to electronic form for Otago was 14 August 2000, with users able to logon and access the database from August 2000. Other offices such as Christchurch, Wellington, Hamilton, and Auckland followed over the next few months and the CR1 implementation was finally completed in mid-2002, *more than two years behind schedule*. Implementation was difficult and users faced continual delays due to problems with the new systems. Survey conversion was not completed until November 2003.

Initial reports on the implementation in Dunedin were remarkably upbeat, noting implementation 'was well-managed, well accepted by users and close to faultless'. The outcome was described as of 'the highest order' (Mallard 2000: 4). However, problems and delays quickly became evident. Completion dates continued to move outwards and EDS faced large penalty payments. EDS was also having problems and delays with software purchased from its subcontractor, Terralink, a state-owned enterprise. Terralink was contracted to develop software that would electronically adjust survey plans. Concerns were raised regarding LINZ's information management group and its ability to provide support to Landonline. In response, an external contractor was employed in early 2000. An Opticon report of 16 June 2000, while generally positive, noted difficulties with EDS's title conversions process and the potential for further delays (Opticon Australia 2000). The title and survey completion process by EDS would continue to run over time.

Processing times fell well behind those achieved by previous manual processes. Approval times for new survey plans rose from five to seven working days to twenty-five, while title plans took twenty working days (Pullar-Strecker 2000). LINZ claimed delays were due to the large number of complex survey plans being lodged and staff adjustment to the new system (Ballard 2000b). Titles and survey conversion were being monitored daily and additional resources were added by EDS and LINZ. Processing problems were still apparent in August, although 95 per cent of registrations of land titles were being completed within eighteen working days. LINZ publicly defended the system, promised to fix the problems, and sent thirty-eight more staff to Dunedin. The chief executive of LINZ, Russ Ballard, responded to the complaints in a letter to the *Dominion* noting that:

> we knew that there would be some initial processing delays as Landonline was rolled out in each land district.
>
> The government recognised this when it agreed to allow a 30 per cent increase in processing times as each office moves from the current paper-based system to one where all our processing is done electronically and we have finished converting that region's records to digital format. The Dunedin implementation is a pilot, and we always knew we were going to have to make operational adjustments.
>
> However, we are positive that, once Landonline is fully implemented in Dunedin, the turnaround times will be at least as good as before, and possibly better.

> Landonline is a world first. No other country has succeeded in combining title and survey in the way Linz has (*Dominion* 2000d).

Throughout 2000 and 2001, problems were discovered with the Informix database, which suffered a series of crashes, the causes of which were sometimes uncertain. These faults required the identification and fixing of bugs, and the introduction of patches and a new version of Informix, which was also found to have problems. An Informix expert was recruited to LINZ on a one-year contract. Informix was purchased by IBM in April 2001, but IBM provided assurances that support for the database would continue. Other bugs were later discovered with software for printing. Due to concerns regarding the ability of LINZ to take on the Landonline programme, a senior LINZ manager was appointed to oversee the transition, and staff with experience of Landonline were seconded to LINZ's Operations Group.

The quality assurance consultant was also becoming uneasy. Opticon raised concerns regarding EDS's testing and their documentation processes, while later reports questioned their level of management expertise and the adequacy of reporting, their ability to develop software and other functions on time, and their lack of energy expended in hiring sufficient staff to carry out conversion functions.

In November 2000, EDS began the survey data conversion project, eight months later than the original contracted date, and delays continued. The conversion project was finally completed two years later than the original contracted date of 31 December 2001. The Surveyors Institute reaffirmed support for the Landonline project at a conference in Queenstown in late August after watching a demonstration of its capabilities. Further staff and resources were made available by both LINZ and EDS. Reporting of problems was now done on a daily basis.

Terralink entered receivership in January 2001, caused mainly by penalties paid as its part of the project ran over time. It was eventually sold in May.[3] In March 2001, EDS employed forty-one former Terralink staff to finish the part of the project that was to have been carried out by Terralink. An agreement between LINZ and the EDS signed on 21 March saw EDS agreeing to complete the survey conversions under the terms of the existing contract, but with a number of concessions made by LINZ to EDS (Robson 2001a). Earlier, EDS had threatened to repudiate the contract.

In the face of the continuing problems, a review of the rollout by Opticon in March 2001 noted that Phase One achieved what it was supposed to, but it was unexpectedly 'resource hungry'. The subsequent report noted:

> whilst [Phase One] has made some simple tasks easier and faster, more complex tasks are generally more difficult and slow.... The net result is that committed and competent staff ... cannot achieve the productivity achieved pre-Landonline (Pullar-Strecker 2001: 1).

The report also recommended management and other changes to some of the computer processes. In addition, it noted the pressure-cooker atmosphere in Dunedin and the 'culture of blame', while many staff had a 'strong perception ... that their problems are not listened to and issues are not resolved either fast enough or decisively enough' (Pullar-Strecker 2001: 1). A post-implementation review of Dunedin and Christchurch in April 2001 noted numerous bugs and small problems. Public reassurances notwithstanding, the quarterly progress report for March–June 2001 also noted operational problems and delays, and LINZ appointed a project manager and convened a steering committee to conduct a post-implementation review of CR1. LINZ considered suing for losses as the damages payable under the contract were reached, but decided to continue with the project. Recommendations of the Opticon report were accepted and implemented, and problems were increasingly dealt with in following months.

By May 2001, 56 per cent of survey plans and 95 per cent of titles were being processed within agreed timeframes, with the averages only slightly behind expected completion times. Implementation began in Wellington in August 2001 and delays continued through early 2002, with processing of new titles taking thirty–thirty-five working days, and sometimes considerably longer. Twenty-five extra staff for twelve months at a cost of $1.125 million were employed to clear backlogs. The Minister of Land Information, Matt Robson, blamed the delays on longer than expected times for staff to become familiar with the system (*Dominion* 2002). Thirty per cent of applications were also being rejected because they had not been filed correctly by lawyers. Claims were made that processing delays, particularly in Wellington, led to the collapse of million-dollar property deals (Howie 2002). During 2001, EDS increased the survey conversion team from forty-one to fifty-seven, then to ninety, and then to 130 to cope with continual delays.

In October 2001, performance of the system worsened again in the face of a number of new bugs and other failures. In November, Landonline was implemented in Hamilton. While the implementation in Auckland was initially to begin in July 2001, several months ahead of schedule, in April the rollout was rescheduled to May 2002. Rollout of Phase One finally began in Auckland in late April 2002. Initial reports were generally positive. Extra staff were employed to deal with large backlogs of transactions, with the cost met by the surplus accumulated from surveyors' title fees and other charges. Incentive schemes were introduced to motivate individual staff performance. High stress levels were noted for those involved in the project.

By December 2001, title transactions were being processed within agreed timeframes, but the majority of survey transactions were still taking too long. The quarterly progress report of December 2001 noted poor performance, but introduced a 'diagnostic tool to monitor transactions and system performance' and the 'enhancement of spatial tools being introduced in the next version of Landonline' (Robson 2001b: 3). By March 2002, processing times in Otago and Southland, by then the only regions where Phase One was complete, were matching pre-Landonline processing times. Staff numbers in Otago and Southland had fallen from fifty-two to thirty-four, plus ten involved in training in preparation for the rollout of Phase Two. However, LINZ continued to warn of further delays and problems throughout 2002, noting in the quarterly progress report of March 2002 that:

A new version of Landonline was implemented on 30/31 March 2002 that was expected to address some of the system performance issues. Initial results indicate there has been no significant improvement in system performance as yet (Robson 2002: 1).

The last paper-based title was issued on 31 May 2002. By 22 September 2002, 94 per cent of titles and 89 per cent of surveys were being processed to the performance standard of twenty and twenty-five working days, respectively. Problems, including stability and slow processing times, continued with the implemented CR1, but were increasingly ironed out over the next years. Title conversion was completed by August 2002. Survey conversion continued into 2003 and was finally completed in November. Despite protests and concerns about access to historical, particularly Treaty-relevant, documents, regional offices were gradually closed, with the last, New Plymouth, closing on 1 February 2002.

Phase Two
The second stage of Landonline was intended to:

enable the electronic lodgement of routine land transfer transactions by conveyancing professionals and the electronic lodgement of the majority of survey transactions by surveyors.

By automating the application of business rules the majority of routine transactions can be processed automatically in real time without manual intervention, and much of the work of validating survey transactions can be [undertaken] automatically (Robson 2001b: 2–3).

Termination of both phases of the Landonline project was being advocated by Treasury in early 1999, as noted. Abandoning the project at the completion of Phase One saw estimated NPV at –$16.7 million. However after completion of Phase Two, NPV was estimated at $58.4 million (CSSECGA 1999: 1). A study in early 1999 concluded that Phase Two was technically feasible and that it could be completed within two years at an estimated cost of $8.2 million. Despite other concerns about completion and timeframes, in May 1999 Treasurer Bill Birch and Finance Minister Bill English met with LINZ officials and agreed to proceed with Phase Two, but only after an 'extensive rethink of the costs and benefits' (*Dominion* 1999b). LINZ consulted with the Law Society and the Institute of Surveyors to conduct what was called a 'reality check' for Phase Two. As LINZ noted, it was encouraged by a 'pretty favourable response' from Birch and English (*Dominion* 1999b).

The new business case, approved by Cabinet on 14 June 1999, estimated a probable cost of $8.5 million and a completion time of two years. It was noted, however, that although 'this forecast is based on a feasibility study, the work for [Phase Two] has not been fully scoped or market tested and therefore there is uncertainty around this forecast' (Ballard 2000: 7). A reassessment of the Landonline business case projected that Phase Two would be completed by August 2002, at a cost of $9.3 million.

Phase Two Begins

The new Labour government, elected in November 1999, quickly made political capital out of the problems Landonline was facing, blaming the previous National government, as they did for INCIS and Health Waikato, and citing Treasury concerns with the project. Monitoring regimes were again tightened. On 21 February 2000, Cabinet established a new ministerial subcommittee which included the Minister of Land Information and Information Technology, the Minister of Finance, and the Minister and Associate Minister of State Services. The aim was to monitor project progress and agree on any contractual commitments over $4 million. LINZ was required to report monthly to the subcommittee and quarterly to the Cabinet Committee on Public Expenditure and Administration. In the face of some concern regarding time and cost risks, a decision was made in December 1999 to divide Phase Two into two parts: an analysis of the user requirements and a fixed-price contract to design and build the system (Swain 2000). LINZ claimed that extending the contract completion date would not undermine completion of the project. As it noted:

> By doing the user requirements study before going to the design and build tender process, we will have a better idea of the scope of that project and how long it might take. However, until we have gone to market, we can't be sure how long it will actually take (Dominion 2000: 4).

The government remained sceptical about the Landonline project, at least publicly, with the State Services Minister Trevor Mallard describing it as a 'major cause of anxiety' and indicating that he was not certain that the second phase of the project would even be rolled out, with the decision to be made before the end of 2000 (*Dominion* 2000). Minister of Information Technology Paul Swain also expressed doubt that Phase Two would continue (Espiner 2000). Despite the rhetoric, the contract for completing user requirements and proof of concept was signed with Andersen Consulting on 1 May 2000 after they had been named as the preferred vendor in early April out of five tenders received (Mallard 2000). This work was estimated to cost between $1.23 million and $1.24 million, with expected completion dates between 6 and 19 October 2000.

In September 2000, LINZ completed the definition of the functional, technical, quality, and usability requirements of Phase Two, and again concluded it was technically feasible to deliver the project. Tender documents for the design and build phase were issued on 19 October. In December, Cabinet agreed to amendments to land title and survey legislation needed to support Phase Two. Of the nine companies that expressed interest in the project, Andersen Consulting (later renamed Accenture), Datacom Systems, EDS New Zealand, HCL Technologies and PwC were invited to tender (*Dominion* 2000a; 2000b). EDS and Datacom declined to submit tenders, EDS stating that it wished to concentrate on completing Phase One, while Datacom did not wish to submit a fixed-price proposal, because of the complexity, size, and technological difficulty of the project.

PwC was chosen as the preferred bidder in February 2001. It provided the least cost bid at between $11 million and $30 million. It was already conducting maintenance for the project and was seen as exposing the Crown to the 'least risk in completing' Phase Two (Robson 2001c: 7). After Cabinet gave approval on 9 April 2001, the contract for the design, build, and implementation of Phase Two was signed on 18 April. The expected cost of the project was fixed at $8.8 million, broken down into lump-sum payments due on the successful completion of the project's components (the milestones). In addition, $1 million was spent on defining user requirements, completed in September 2000, while $0.3 million was set aside for LINZ to cover costs such as hardware and software, project and change management and so forth (Robson 2001a). The most likely total cost was estimated at $13.1 million. It was proposed that routine title transactions – around 50 per cent of all transactions – would be processed automatically, in real time without intervention from LINZ. Paul Swain, the Minister of Information Technology, noted on 3 April 2001 that LINZ chief executive Russ Ballard would be held to account over the success or failure of the project. Expectations were great regarding the project, with the LINZ chief executive noting, 'I can see the day when Linz could well become a virtual agency' (*Dominion* 2001).

Problems with Phase Two
The design and build part of Phase Two was expected to be completed by February 2002. Later estimates saw 28 September 2002 as the completion date (Robson 2001a). Delays and problems were apparent from the start, expected completion dates continued to move outwards, and Phase Two was finally completed in November 2003. There were considerable tensions between LINZ and PwC. As an August 2001 report noted:

LINZ is not satisfied with all the work PwC has done to date and this is creating some tension…This has led to significant debate with PwC over the quality of the staff who are working on this part of the project (Usherwood 2001: 4).

By early 2002, the pilot was also several months late, and LINZ noted in February that it was 'concerned that PwC is falling significantly behind on its plan to complete CR2 by 20 May 2002.' PwC did not accept this assessment (Ballard 2002: 2). Opticon also expressed scepticism regarding some of PwC's progress reports, noting that they were 'unrealistic', did not 'reflect the "on the ground" realities' and failed to 'demonstrate insight and experience' (Opticon 2002: 11). Opticon also noted problems with the level of management expertise and experience at PwC. In October, PwC (by now purchased by IBM) admitted software was not up to scratch. PwC disputed some damages claimed by LINZ, and in response a price reduction was negotiated for the contracts. After further delays and the redesign and rebuild of one of its components, Phase Two was finally completed in November 2003, as noted above.

The expected cost of the total project was reiterated as $146 million and, although there were considerable time overruns, LINZ managed to keep the project within this revised budget, largely because of the fixed price contracts and the damages paid by the suppliers for the delays. Costs for Phase Two were $12.561 million, less than the $15.1 million approved by Cabinet in April 2001. In October 2002, LINZ notified that the annual operating costs of Landonline were likely to be $3–4 million more than expected, and chief executive Russ Ballard requested an increase in LINZ's baseline funding from the Cabinet. LINZ requested another $27–36 million over nine years, blaming the funding shortfall on bigger than expected forecasts of technology expenses and reductions in savings from job cuts being less than expected (Pullar-Strecker 2002).

Roll-out of Phase Two

Once Phase Two was approved by the government, roll-out began in the South Island and followed in the North Island. In Canterbury, Phase Two, built by PwC, was piloted in November 2002–February 2003 by a group of thirty surveyors and law firms, although the initial pilot had been planned for October. The first reports after the project went live described only minor problems. However, by March 2003, problems were reported with the software used to electronically generate survey plans (called eSurvey) and it was ultimately redesigned and rebuilt. Delays continued. The eDealings component of Landonline, rolled out in March in the South Island and April 2003 in the North Island, allowed lawyers to securely access LINZ's land registry and lodge and discharge mortgages and title transfers, without recourse to paper documents or the intervention of LINZ staff. It also led to significant falls in fees for transferring land titles and altering mortgages. While many lawyers and others were impressed by the new system, the Law Society expressed some concern at the lack of training available for users. Even with positive assessments by professional groups, several months after the implementation of eDealings only 1–2 per cent of routine title transactions were being lodged electronically, and many of these were between professionals in the same organisation. In August, Russ Ballard was replaced by Brendan Boyle as chief executive of LINZ. The redesigned and rebuilt electronic survey – eSurvey – was finally implemented on 3 November 2003.

Project Completion

By late 2003, LINZ reports on Landonline were generally positive, although the Audit Office noted problems with the uptake of electronic lodgement and some performance issues (Audit Office 2003). In September, LINZ's call centre had received the Telecommunication Users Association of NZ's Contact Centre Innovation of the Year Award. Despite initial problems, stability and performance of the system had improved by November 2003. A delegation from Australia visited to examine Landonline's performance. However, LINZ faced continuing difficulties in encouraging the use of the Landonline system, which remained extremely low, considerably undermining its expected NPV. Revised estimates for titles take-up in November 2003 were 19.2 per cent in 2003/4 and 47 per cent in 2004/5, and survey 'up-takes' of 5 per cent in 2003/4 and 25 per cent in 2004/5. Reasons for low levels of 'up-take' were given as 'resistance to change', 'concerns about system stability' and 'retention of paper system' (Audit Office 2003: 18). The new chief executive argued that this reluctance to embrace new systems and electronic transactions was also partly because the overheated residential market meant customers were busy with conveyancing work and had limited time to 'learn something new in terms of the operation of Landonline' (Primary Production Committee 2003: 3). This excuse would be reiterated in 2005. As a large part of the net present value of the project depended on the take-up by professionals, LINZ engaged in a strategy to increase usage of the system, including marketing it, and providing training and after-sales support.

By November 2003, the estimated net present value of the system had fallen to $13.1 million. The final cost was $138.7 million. Seventy per cent of land transactions could be processed automatically but professionals remained highly reluctant to use the system, with only 5 per cent of land titles and 1.5 per cent of survey documents being filed electronically. In somewhat of an understatement, LINZ's general manager of operations, Sharon Cottrell, noted this level of usage was 'lower than forecast' (*Dominion Post* 2004: 10). Discussions continued regarding the updating of some of the now ageing technology upon which Landonline was based, such as the optical disks used to store land records, and the use of the Informix database, the future of which was in doubt after being purchased by IBM in 2001, although IBM continued to support the system. New server and disk hardware were installed in a $1.2m 'technical refresh' under the facilities management contract with EDS. This went live in mid-March 2005. Usage grew slowly and steadily, but was still well below initial expectations. As the Primary Production Committee (2005: 2) noted, the 'target for e-capable transactions was 23 per cent for the 2004/05 financial year but as at May 2005, only 7.8 per cent had been achieved.' By June 2005, 25.5 per cent of all surveys lodged were Landonline e-surveys. Improvements, upgrades, and bug fixing continued.

By December 2005 22 per cent of titles and 37 per cent of survey transactions were lodged electronically. In February 2006 the Government announced that by 1 July 2008 all survey and title transactions were to be lodged electronically. Further staff savings and the closure of all regional offices by 2015 – with the exception of Hamilton and Christchurch – were announced.

Conclusion: Was Landonline a Success?

The evaluation of Landonline by Teega Associates in June 2003 – before Phase Two was actually completed – was generally positive. As it argued:

LINZ can rightly claim they have delivered a successful program based on the 1999 reviews. The program delivered within this revised budget and there was a projected positive financial benefit together with unqualified benefits within the user communities.

... the value of this conversion of data to digital form cannot be underestimated as to future value. As an analogy, conversion of paper-based banking systems allowed an unchanged mechanism going back decades if not centuries to radically reinvent its processes and extended into unforeseeable activities (at the time of conversion) (Teega Associates Ltd 2003: 7).

Teega were sceptical that the net present value measurement used could capture the long-term benefits of the conversion. They argued that at some stage LINZ would have had to convert its paper-based systems to digital ones. Full time staff members decreased from 821 in 1997 to 587 by the end of 2003, which delivered most of the financial benefits directly accruing to LINZ. Teega, however, also noted a number of problems with the system, including the 'limited number of users', the 'considerable manual intervention' still required, and the freezing of technology during the development process in the face of rapid technological change. They also expressed strong reservations about the poor performance of IBM (including the former PwC) and EDS in some areas, and the continual reliance of LINZ on EDS for facilities management and IBM for maintenance.

In the *Inquiry for the Requisition Rate for Survey Plans* in May 2003, Landonline received a mixture of praise and brickbats from the surveyors interviewed. Surveyors noted data 'is more accessible for firms outside the main centres, and there is a significant saving in time spent on searching … Landonline has made it [easier for some] to prepare and deposit their data sets' (Tanner 2003: 13). But the system was also seen as considerably 'slower than anticipated', rigid, and 'unforgiving' and there were problems with some of the images scanned – and to return to the original was costly and difficult. Pressure on processing items led some to conclude quality had suffered. There were also concerns about the lack of context and local knowledge in the system, and skill deficits and inflexibility amongst LINZ staff; eSurvey was seen as difficult to use.

In December 2003, the new chief executive, Brendan Boyle, was upbeat about the project. He reported to the Primary Production Committee (2003: 4) that:

> we've achieved a lot of productivity gains since the system came in. I talked about the white-hot property market. We've got a twenty percent increase in transactions over forecast. We've had a reduced number of staff, the closure of offices, and the system has proven to be very effective in enabling us to manage the workload, in that we have consistently met or exceeded the performance targets, despite the significant increase in volume. So that is testimony to the effectiveness of the system.

However, committee members were sceptical about reported NPVs, given the low use of the electronic transactions. They also noted the lack of easy access to local paper-based, particularly historical, documents in a climate where historical claims regarding land and confiscation issues remains a live issue. While there was access through the Internet-based Skylight system, customers had to have some knowledge of the document and know, according to a LINZ witness, 'exactly what they're looking for' and had to be a subscriber to the system (Primary Production Committee 2003).

In 2004, LINZ saw the project as a success with 'all live and cancelled certificates of title, and approximately 70% of surveyed land parcels … in electronic form … accessible from remote locations' (LINZ 2004). Fees were lower than they had been for the previous manual process. While survey transactions still require some manual processing, LINZ 'undertakes to process survey transactions lodged as electronic datasets within 10 working days which is 50% shorter' than manual processes (LINZ 2004). The automation of the discharge, transfer, and mortgage title processes allows instant registration, compared to the previous fifteen days of manual processing. But even LINZ acknowledged technical success had not necessarily translated to use, with the popularity of its searching functions – according to LINZ 99.2 per cent of land record searches are carried out electronically – not matched by the use of its more sophisticated transactional functions, some of which remained at very low levels. Given its projected NPV is dependent on usage, this remains a concern.

In sum, if Landonline was a success, it was certainly a marginal one and the completion of the project was touch-and-go for much of its lifetime. Some measures of project success – including a number of the standard ones already discussed such as the strict success criteria on-time and on-budget of its initial business case – rate Landonline a failure. The majority of intended users did not use the more sophisticated aspects of the system by mid-2005, a year and a half after it was considered completed, so even with its technical achievement, its success as a function of user-acceptance remains doubtful. Abandonment was considered in 1999 and advocated by Treasury. It is at least questionable in retrospect that a government would have approved a projected $141 million investment (or, for that matter, the original estimate of $95 million) for a system that may not have worked; with a high risk of political fallout if it failed; with major functions still unused by some of its intended clients; and with the NPV a fraction of that originally predicted and still uncertain. Nor, again in retrospect, would a government be as likely to have approved a system delivered years later than predicted, with technology already approaching obsolescence. While Phase Two and the relaunched project were delivered within the revised budget and fixed price contracts, as Treasury noted, this may have been because there was considerable slack in the design of the contracts and the project was over-costed – and the contracts were not successful in constraining time overrun, despite the heavy penalty payments.[4] However, having said that, LINZ considers the development was worthwhile and to some extent inevitable, even despite problems. If it is true that LINZ at some stage would be required to convert its paper-based data to digital forms, then the low and rather uncertain financial returns from the project may in future be seen to be justified. However, it is possible that delaying the project for a number of years until technology improved may have increased the likelihood of a better financial return and decreased the likelihood that the project would fail altogether. On the other hand, further delays would have led to further increases in paper-based documents filling further kilometres of shelves. As such, at very best, Landonline can be seen as a partial success, a glass half full – or half empty – depending on your point of view. This may be the most we can hope for from a large project.

7.

Lessons from Computer Development in the New Zealand Public Sector

ICT disasters in the New Zealand public sector, some examined in previous chapters, illustrate the problems of enthusiam and control that make failure of large projects difficult to avoid. Largely in response to these disasters, New Zealand public sector ICT monitoring mechanisms moved away from being highly decentralised and laissez-faire regimes to become increasingly prescriptive by the early 2000s. We examine these regimes and draw lessons from our case studies, before arguing for a degree of pessimism in ICT development. The key monitoring agencies are the State Services Commission, with a watching brief over the entire public sector; Treasury, which guards the public purse; and the Department of the Prime Minister and Cabinet, which represents, as its name suggests, the interests of the Prime Minister and Cabinet. The Office of the Controller and Auditor-General also maintains a watching brief over the public sector and the public purse for Parliament, and has commented, often unfavourably, on ISDs in the public sector. In the health sector, much of which sits beyond the core public sector, monitoring continues to involve these agencies as well as the Ministry of Health, District Health Boards, and Primary Health Organisations.

The INCIS and Health Waikato SMS projects were conceived within required standards as outlined in the 1991 *Review of Computing in the State Sector* and subsequent *Getting the Bits Right* (State Services Commission 1991; 1992). Central monitoring of departmental and public hospital ICT projects was minimal at the time. The Computer Services Division of the State Services Commission, established in 1970, had had its control of state-sector ICT role separated from its service provider role in 1979/80, after well-publicised problems with health ICT systems. After another review in 1985, the Computer Services Division was separated from the State Services Commission and renamed Government Computing Services. This was made a state-owned enterprise in 1987 and privatised in 1994. After this, government agencies made their own provisions for ICT and were largely left to their own devices, at least until problems became too big to ignore.

For much of the 1990s, ICT project monitoring was regarded as a straightforward reporting and auditing matter. No consideration was given to the special problems of ICT projects, such as the difficulty of measuring progress. Nor were controlling cost blow-outs, or making these blow-outs grounds for terminating a project, considered. Quality assurance was treated as an internal departmental (or, as in the health sector, commissioning organisational) matter – something that became problematic in the INCIS, Health Waikato, and other disasters where internal mechanisms largely failed. As such, there was little effective control and monitoring of ICT projects by either Treasury, the State Services Commission, or the Ministry of Health over the health sector. In the case of INCIS, this was problematic as the Police are not part of the core public service (and therefore removed from the control of the central agencies) and are largely governed by their own Act of Parliament, the Police Act 1958. In December 1997, the Police INCIS project agreed to comply voluntarily with the monitoring regime, and sent copies of their internal and independent audit reports to the State Services Commission for the December 1997 and March 1998 quarters. In May 1998 Cabinet directed that INCIS be subjected to the monitoring regimes conducted by the State Services Commission and, on 12 June 1998, the State Services Commission wrote to the Police reiterating this. However, even with this direct and active monitoring, Police reporting was misleading and often fictional. Health Waikato presented a similar situation, with the CHE board responsible for project commissioning and monitoring. Central government belatedly concerned itself with the SMS purchase, employing consultants to investigate, but lacked power to intervene in board decisions. Furthermore, it sent a series of mixed messages that served to confuse the decision-making process.

The INCIS failure and other problems encouraged a series of reports and inquiries, and considerable rewriting of procurement and accountability mechanisms. These became more prescriptive over time. The *Information Technology Stocktake* (State Services Commission 1997) was largely supportive of existing arrangements, but further alarming disclosures led to the establishment of an ad hoc committee of public service officials, chaired by the State Services Commission, after a Cabinet decision of July 1997. This was to monitor large ICT projects and report to Cabinet. In November 1999, in response to further problems, another ad hoc review of public sector ICT was initiated. Reports were commissioned from the SIMPL group (SIMPL/NZIER 2000) and the Office of the Auditor-General (Macdonald 2000). SIMPL was generally positive regarding ISD in the public sector and reported:

> the New Zealand public sector would appear to be meeting international and local performance standards in terms of managing IT projects [and] there is little support for the notion that there is any systemic problem associated particularly with New Zealand public sector IT management (SIMPL/NZIER 2000: 12).

The Auditor-General's report was less positive and made a considerable number of recommendations. The recommendations of these reports, a number of Cabinet circulars and other studies, and the recommendations of the ministerial inquiry into

INCIS (see Chapter 5), were incorporated into requirements for a revised regime for the approval and monitoring of large ICT projects produced by the State Services Commission and others in 2001 (Cabinet Office 2001; Small 2000; State Services Commission 2001).

The central agencies' monitoring role was affirmed for major projects, as was their responsibility for setting guidelines for procurement and management of projects. The accountability of chief executives for the overall success of projects was reaffirmed. Major projects were those:

- with projected life cycle costs of $15 million or more
- that included a project capital investment of $7 million or more
- whose failure would expose the Crown or departments to significant risks
- that involved more than one agency
- directed by the minister to be monitored by the central agencies.

Departments were required to provide independent quality assurance and send these to the monitoring agencies, as well as to notify them of any change in the management or specifications of the project. One of the key recommendations was that projects be broken down into modules or milestones for development, with each considered an independent business case. Approval of new projects subsequently required a two-step process. The first step was getting approval for developing detailed costs and proposed benefits, based on initial indicative projections. The final approval depended on a consideration of these more fully developed projections of costs and benefits. A presumption was given to the use of existing technology in developments, and the use of a quantitative risk analysis model was prescribed.

Problems with the New Monitoring Regime

While an improvement on what has gone before, the new prescriptions still suffer from a belief that project failure could be avoided largely by setting in place the right monitoring regime, the right contract design, and using the required risk analysis mechanisms. There was a presumption given to using existing technology, but this was not as forceful as it should have been. In any event, the SMS purchases at Health Waikato and Capital Coast Health were propelled by an apparent ministerial directive that 'off-the-shelf' products be purchased. Failure still occurred. The most glaring problem with the new regime was that, while highly prescriptive regarding procurement techniques and contract design, it did not address the major problem underpinning computer failure: that of a continuing overwhelming enthusiasm for ICT. Still unacknowledged is the lesson of decades of failure: *large projects generally fail*. Breaking these projects into milestones and separate contracts may go some way towards mitigating this problem – but does not dispel it. A large project, with a long timeframe of development and high expectations for the benefits it will deliver, is still a large project even if broken down into smaller contracts and milestones. Indeed, splitting projects up creates its own tensions, and interoperability of different components remains a problem.

Despite continual failure, large projects are still initiated in the New Zealand public sector. In late 2001, the ACC initiated a $173 million project, dwarfing INCIS. Figures for the proposed upgrade of the Ministry of Social Development's SWIFTT system, after years of discussion, ranged between $78 million and $180 million – with some commentators placing the costs as high as $500 million – while the Ministry refused for a while to release cost projections, citing commercial confidentiality (*Computer World* 2004). In addition, the highly prescriptive requirements regarding procurement can be ignored by departments: the $173 million ACC contract was awarded to UNISYS without calling for tenders (Hosking 2002). UNISYS was already carrying out significant work for the ACC, suggesting some degree of supplier capture was possible.

Contracts

The overwhelming and naive reliance on a flawed contract, which was signed before major issues were settled and later revised, was a feature of the INCIS fiasco. Flawed contracts have also been a factor in other failures. Reviews of the Health Waikato SMS contract concluded it failed to give sufficient detail of what the vendor would provide. The contract was hastily signed without ensuring appropriate product support, and it failed to protect Health Waikato from any changes in the SMS product. This left Health Waikato responsible for maintaining a potentially obsolete and unsupported system when SMS announced that it would be discontinuing a core module. Contracts, fundamental to public sector organisation through the 1990s (and today), also failed to provide a foundation for effective IS development across New Zealand's health sector.

The design of the Landonline contracts, particularly in the relaunched project, reflected lessons from INCIS and elsewhere, as well as the new accountability and monitoring regimes being developed in the wake of ongoing disasters. As such, Landonline provides a partial test of the new regimes. Proof of concept and design and build phases, and management of the systems, were let as separate contracts. There was contestability in software packages and hardware, as opposed to the developers of the system also providing the hardware at full retail price, as happened with INCIS. Contracts themselves were divided into milestones, with payment contingent on completion of milestones and with penalty payments for lateness. The separation of design contracts and build contracts is intuitively appealing, but has risks of its own. In the case of the separation of the design and build contracts for Phase One, the same firm (PwC) that designed the project later claimed it was unable to build from its own design. Some contracts, initially designed as contestable, were rolled into one – with the results that EDS was providing facilities management and hardware as well as carrying out data conversion, provoking some annoyance from other tenderers. Like most purchasers, LINZ was unable to commit the parties to guaranteeing interoperability of the different components, which meant it bore the risks if interoperability ever became a serious issue. The array of numerous and complex contracts can become rather confusing in itself. Contract design is not a panacea for problems of failure.

Problems of contestability remain in a market where there are few suppliers. Fujitsu, who supplied Health Waikato's IS prior to (and after) the SMS purchase, initially showed little interest in continuing to provide or further develop its product. This is possibly because of the difficulties it had encountered in building and maintaining the Hospro-W system. Only a small number of vendors were ever interested in tendering for the Health Waikato project, and Health Waikato put considerable effort into stimulating supplier interest in their desire for a new IS. There appeared, of course, to be no shortage of consultants available to provide opinions on Health Waikato's 'needs' and various IS offerings.

The Landonline project also shows how concentration amongst IT companies and consultancies can reduce competition, particularly in such a small market as New Zealand. This concentration increased during the life of the project. During the development, IBM purchased PwC – a company that it had been in competition with during the tendering for the project. Another IBM purchase was Accenture, formerly Andersen Consulting, responsible for developing the proof of concept of Phase Two. The Informix database also joined the IBM family, and for a while there were anxieties regarding its continued existence. In addition, concerns were expressed by Teega that LINZ was in danger of being held captive by IBM (formerly PwC), for as well as developing a large part of Landonline, IBM was contracted to maintain it. This contract was valid until October 2005. Reviews of the Health Waikato SMS purchase highlighted the fact that the succession of consultants providing advice to Health Waikato meant that no single agent had a clear picture of Health Waikato's needs. Indeed, government agencies can be overly dependent on private consultants, companies, and competing tenderers to supply computer expertise and to provide auditing and checks on other private companies. These companies may cease to be competitors or even independent consultants during the lifetime of the project. To protect themselves against consultant and supplier capture, or incapacity to provide coherency through the lifetime of a project, governments and commissioning organisations need a considerable degree of capacity and expertise in information system development. It is questionable whether this exists in the New Zealand state sector. Governments also need to ensure departments at least attempt contestability – as noted, the $173 million ACC contract was awarded without competitive tendering.

The length of projects, as well as size, also remains a problem. While the Landonline project was broken down into milestones and separate contracts, the size and length of the project still presented considerable risks. By the time it was considered completed in late 2003, continual delays had undermined its net present value, and rendered some of its technological components nearly obsolete. While penalty payments were made for lateness, it is possible that suppliers had built these into their projected costs from the start, in which case the project was possibly over-costed. It should be noted that this long timeframe was not only the result of delays – the original project had a completion period of several years. Long development timeframes can also be at greater risk of legislative changes. For example, the INCIS project director claimed changes to the legal requirements for INCIS increased costs by millions of dollars. A key lesson of Landonline and other projects is that long-term IS developments should be generally avoided, as the risks of failure, technological obsolescence, legislative change, and cost and time overruns are markedly increased. Short-term and somewhat unadventurous developments are considerably less risky, if less exciting.

Monitoring and Accountability Problems

However active the monitoring regime, the case studies in this book demonstrate that problems will continue. Even after the central agencies, ministers, and Parliament became involved in the monitoring of INCIS, the Police consistently assured them that the project was progressing well. During 1997/8, the Justice and Law Reform Select Committee reported that most of 'the responses to us from the Police were positive in outlook and conveyed, particularly with regard to INCIS, an impression that everything was on track' (Waitai 1999). Police did not report at all to Cabinet between January 1996 and January 1998. Even when reporting, the Police were not always entirely co-operative with monitoring agencies or Parliament and reports continued to be misleading. As the select committee noted:

> issues of commercial sensitivity continued through the lifetime of the INCIS project. If we had accepted the Police's position, we would effectively have been accepting that no IT project in any department within our terms of reference could be subject to in-depth scrutiny by the committee (Waitai 1999).

In an environment dominated by contracts and contracting out, claims of commercial sensitivity may continue to be used as a useful shield behind which problems can be concealed.

As a result of lessons from the INCIS experience and elsewhere, monitoring of the Landonline project reached high levels, and regular reporting and external quality assurance was required, particularly in the relaunched project. Any spending over $4 million had to be approved by a ministerial sub-committee, which also required monthly reports. However, external quality assurance consultants Opticon did express considerable scepticism over the accuracy of some reporting by the developers, and often reassurances regarding delivery times turned out to be optimistic. As noted in Chapter 1, however prescriptive the monitoring requirements, there will always be doubts about the accuracy of progress reports due to the very nature of complex IS developments where progress is difficult to measure, different cultures talk past each other, and there are problems of agency.

Ministerial Accountability and Responsibility

Accountability remains a problem in ISDs, whatever the monitoring regime. In a Westminster system such as New Zealand, ministers hold a vicarious responsibility for the decisions and omissions of their departments and the employees of their departments, in theory at least. That this vicarious responsibility, let alone the personal responsibility of the minister for his or her own actions and duties, is not taken as seriously as some constitutional scholars would prefer, and may have been undermined somewhat by the application of NPM in the New Zealand public sector, has been much commented on (Gregory 1998). It is a principle that still has some force, however, at least amongst some voters and scholars. However, in complex IS projects that may last several years, there may be a number of changes of ministers. Ministers may or may not be aware of the project and any problems it is facing, and so may not be in a position to ameliorate any of the effects. As illustrated in Chapter 3, there was a succession of ministers and health information strategies from the early 1990s onwards; each time similar problems arose, and each time attempts to provide leadership, continuity or coherency failed. Nor was anyone ultimately accountable for failures. During INCIS there was a procession of four different police ministers, which made accountability difficult. When things became too bad to ignore, a special Ministerial Group was established, containing senior ministers from various portfolios. Some rather prescient cautions were raised by Maurice Williamson, the Minister of Information Technology, early in the INCIS project, but he was assured these would be addressed. Nor in the age of NPM was it usual for ministers to intimately involve themselves in the operational matters of their departments until problems become too large and politically damaging to ignore. Thus, when a project fails, it may be difficult to hold one individual minister responsible, even if that minister was intimately involved in and approved the original project. It might be easier to pin the blame on a particular government – as the Labour government after 1999 has tried to do in the cases of INCIS, the SMS failures at Health Waikato and Capital Coast Health, and the fiasco of health sector ISDs through the 1990s. However, if it is difficult to ascribe blame for dramatic disasters that have a seemingly simple cause–effect relationship (Gregory 1998), it is more difficult to hold ministers and governments to account for highly complex development projects where it is difficult to explain why failure occurred, let alone who is responsible.

Chief Executives and Other Managers

If conventions of ministerial responsibility provide little hope for accountability – not to mention for the control of projects – could the chief executive, senior manager, or project sponsor be in a position to avoid project failure and be held to account should things go wrong? Treasury (2000) and other agencies reaffirmed chief executive accountability for the success or otherwise of projects, while noting the difficulty of holding these people accountable for the delivery of every module. Much is also made of the role of the chief executive in project success. The Teega evaluation of Landonline (Teega Associates Ltd 2003) sees the contribution of Russ Ballard, the chief executive of LINZ, as central to the successful completion of Landonline, and argues that the strong commitment of the chief executive and/or project sponsor is vital in the successful completion of a project. This commitment can become a double-edged sword, however. As we have already discussed in Chapter 1, there are considerable problems of agency and reluctance of developers and others to report bad news. If a manager is strongly linked with the project itself, there may be a reluctance to admit to bad news or to curtail the project. Police Commissioner Peter Doone was highly identified, and identified himself, with the INCIS project, and continued to reassure outside monitoring authorities the project was on track. Doone was the project sponsor for most of the INCIS project. He was a highly qualified technocrat, with a Master of Public Policy from Harvard University (from a Harkness Fellowship in 1985) and twenty-seven years' experience of policing (Bain 1996). He was also a strong proponent of the 'community policing' to be supported by the new system (see Doone 1989) and remained a defender of INCIS to the end. When the entire INCIS project was being redesigned from the ground up, he wrote to *North and South* claiming 'less paperwork and streamlined procedures will follow with the introduction of new technology, including INCIS. The new systems are late but they are coming in' (Doone 1997). Similarly, Project Manager Tony Crewdson was an initiator of and strongly linked with the project and assured doubters as to its status. He, too, was accused of not keeping enough distance between himself and the IBM suppliers (Waitai 1999).

On the other hand, despite many attempts to find someone to pin the blame on for ICT failures (and the tendency to sometimes characterise ICT failures as largely caused by stupidity or lack of management skills amongst certain individuals), processes are often so complex, with so many players, that it is difficult to reduce failures simply to the limitations of key individuals. This was certainly true of the Health Waikato failure, where a tangled path of events and a wide range of players were involved. Apportioning blame can take on the characteristics of scapegoating, where the involvement and failings of consultants, suppliers, external monitoring agencies, and so on, are sidelined by focusing attention and blame on a few or on one individual. Some of the comments made in various documents about the project director of INCIS – only one player amongst many – show such tendencies towards scapegoating. What is remarkable is that the IT companies that ran the project, and the consultancy companies that supported it and its over-blown expectations, reviewed it, and recommended that it continue with better management processes in the face of continuing difficulties, seem to have escaped sanction. Indeed, many were subsequently employed on later government projects. Scapegoating was also evident in the Health Waikato fiasco, with fingers pointed at, among others, Health Waikato Board Chair Jack Jenkins, and CCMAU. In sum, whatever the accountability mechanisms, it is unlikely they will solve the problem of failure.

Enthusiastic Projections and Idolisation

We have noted at length the fanciful benefit, time, and cost projections of the INCIS project, and the 'idolisation' of ICT by the Police. However, regardless of the lessons of INCIS and other failures, even in putative successes, projections have often been over-enthusiastic and erroneous. Despite claims made regarding the conservatism of the NPV projections for Landonline, for example, initial forecasts for the usage, cost, and completion timeframe of the Landonline system were considerably optimistic. Doubts raised by external consultants regarding completion times were, in some instances, strongly disputed by LINZ and Opticon. When termination of the project was being considered in 1999, LINZ still maintained an unwarranted optimism regarding completion times and expected NPV. Completion times for the project were optimistic even in the relaunched project. In Health Waikato's case, the board maintained a preference for, and then swiftly entered into contract with, SMS – despite suggestions from various consultants and clinical staff that its product would not fulfil needs.

Even putatively successful projects may find themselves underused, further undermining optimistic projections. Project and systems success may not lead to user success. Usage of Landonline's more sophisticated functions remained well below that expected, considerably lowering its projected NPV. This reiterates one of the key findings of other studies of ICT failure and e-government: whatever the technical excellence of a development, its success can be undermined if customers and/or employees are reluctant to use the system. Users may be happy to use simple searching functions, but are more reluctant to use complex transactional functions. The enthusiasm for technology found amongst software developers and some public servants is not necessarily shared by professionals and citizens, particularly if they are sceptical of the benefits. The considerable costs of learning new systems, new skills, and changing work practices may make people reluctant to use new computer systems, even if they *can* see future benefits. The difficulty of learning the new Landonline systems was indeed commented on by professionals, and LINZ has devoted considerable resources to training, as well as to the promotion of the new system. Some professionals may have been simply resistant to and resentful of change, even if it seemed to provide benefits and was supported by their professional associations. This user-resistance should not be forgotten when making projections about the financial and other benefits of new computer developments.

Lomanism and Managerial Faddism

Enthusiasm of ICT salespeople for their products – what we termed lomanism in Chapter 1 – remains a danger for public sector developments. In the case of INCIS, the degree of drop-out and scepticism of nearly all initial tenderers for the project – some such as Marconi and Andersen Consulting were aware that the Police requirements were unrealistic and unachievable – was not matched by IBM's continual enthusiasm for the project and persistent reassurances on their ability to deliver the INCIS requirements. That this solution was to be delivered through IBM proprietary software, and IBM hardware provided largely at retail price against what was seen as normal practice even then in ISDs, possibly reflected the salesmanship of IBM employees. Whether the unwillingness of IBM to strongly caution Police that their expectations of ICT were unrealistic, given Police naivety about ISDs in general, was a genuine mistake on the part of IBM, or a stated (or unstated) sales technique remains an open question, but such behaviour seems to have been replicated in other failures. For their part, the Police, who had limited skill or experience in ISD, possibly overestimated their own expertise in ICT. While overselling by SMS did not determine the Health Waikato purchase, SMS failed to ensure Health Waikato had defined its IS needs, or to warn of possible difficulties in adapting a system designed for North American health care to the New Zealand context.

Managerial faddism was also a problem in the INCIS and Health Waikato failures. With INCIS, complexity was considerably increased by a restructuring underpinned by a then popular fad 'Business Process Re-engineering',[1] and the related Community Policing Project (Policing 2000), all closely linked to the ultimately failed INCIS system. This complexity was a problem from the start and in February 1996, the Deputy Commissioner of Police and the Secretary to Treasury wrote to their respective ministers seeking an extension of time for reporting, due to the difficulties of the reorganisation. INCIS and Policing 2000 were initially planned as being intertwined, with Business Process Engineering, to use the jargon of the time, seeking:

> a dramatic improvement in performance. It focuses an organisation on customer services and analyses processes in terms of value of the service to the customer. It develops a vision of future performance for each process, and eliminates, combines, simplifies or replaces activities, or whole processes, which are not adding optimum value. BPR uses technology, particularly IT, as an enabler of performance improvement. It relies on the introduction of rigorous performance measurement as a guide to both initial and ongoing performance improvements (Luxton 1995: 10–11).

While it was stated in bold print that 'Policing 2000 is not about job cuts' (Luxton 1995: 9), it initially involved the planned 'downsizing' of 500 positions, ultimately not carried out due to political pressure. Health Waikato's SMS purchase and implementation was also intimately linked to 'organisational re-engineering', with an assumption that clinical staff would simply adapt to the new system and suitably redesign their work processes. For an organisation to embrace a management fad and carry out restructuring at the same time as it is developing an interlinked, complex, and ultimately failed ISD, does seem to be of questionable wisdom. But it is not unusual in ICT failures.

Faddism continues in the public sector. E-government may simply be the latest in a succession of public administration trends. As noted in Chapter 2, it has been embraced by the advanced world's governments with claims that cost savings, efficiencies, public sector downsizing, and enhanced citizen participation in the business of government will result. The jury, of course, is still out on whether e-government will deliver on its claimed benefits. Much has also been made of the quantitative risk analysis used in Landonline and its role in the putative success of the project. It is a prescription of the new ISD regimes in the public sector. The graphs and percentages generated certainly imbue projections with a comforting air of scientific exactitude . However, this is not a scientific objectivity greatly deserved, as projections are largely based on the more-or-less educated guesses of 'experts'. That such educated guesses are quantified and graphed does not mean they are any less subjective, inexact, and prone to error. In any event, projections regarding completion times generally turned out to be somewhat inaccurate in Landonline: sometimes by years. What reliability they had was often as much a matter of luck, good judgement, or the design of the contracts as fixed price ones, which meant cost overruns were borne by the suppliers. It should also be noted no other projects have been halted because of the use of the model. The prescribed risk analysis again shows elements of managerial faddism, where new techniques are adopted with great enthusiasm and confidence, but without a great deal of evidence of efficacy. The continued dependence of the New Zealand public sector on external consultants whose culture and livelihood is inherently tied up with the adoption and marketing of the latest management fad means faddism remains an ever-present danger.

Furthermore, the degree of change a new computer system can make to an organisation, particularly if it is linked with a reorganisation, should not be underestimated. This can be for good or ill – and change does not necessarily bring benefits, despite the often strong beliefs of management consultants and managerial fads to that end. The original aim of Landonline was to automate the manual processes of LINZ. However, once the new system was in place, work processes were found to be fundamentally overhauled. Again, while this is seen to have positive benefits for LINZ, such fundamental change increases the risks and uncertainties of a development. As noted in one interview by the authors:

All Landonline set out to do was to automate the manual processes, but now that it has been going a few years nearly the whole of LINZ has been re-engineered. If we had known everything that was going to happen at the beginning of the project then we would never have started it – it would have been too scary.

Radical change in itself can be costly and disruptive with benefits uncertain. The Landonline development led to several years of considerable disruption, both for LINZ and professionals using the system. Stress levels for those involved in developing and implementing the system were high. Such disruption and tensions can easily be forgotten in the euphoria of success when a project is finally finished, but have real fiscal and other costs that should not be overlooked.

Front-line Staff and User Acceptance

Front-line staff might well be able to provide a 'reality check' on IS developers and management, but in the bureaucracies and systems of top-down management found in NPM, user and employer resistance can be ignored. The Health Waikato chief executive resigned shortly after delivering a report, rejected by the board, that showed clinical opposition to the SMS system. Clinical staff continued to air their concerns about the SMS purchase and were relieved when the project was abandoned, although aggrieved at the loss of money that could have been allocated to clinical services. Throughout the purchase process, consultation with clinical and other hospital staff – the main users of SMS – was limited.

Similarly, the widespread opposition to INCIS did not stop or contain it. There were perfunctory efforts in convincing the front-line police that INCIS had benefits for them, but there was generally great scepticism amongst them towards both the INCIS project and the Community Policing Project (and opposition to projected job cuts) to which it was linked. Greg O'Conner, the head of the Police Association during most of the INCIS fiasco, claimed that the Community Policing Strategy had undermined the effectiveness of front-line police, undervalued 'firm but fair police officers' respected by the criminal fraternity, led to the dominance of the Police force by 'academics', used up valuable resources, and reduced the overall effectiveness of the Police force (Coddington 2001). Dave Wilkinson, an ex-policeman, noted in an interview in *North and South* that 'if there's a pub fight a computer isn't going to stop you getting bottled' (Chamberlain 1997). In the unlikely event of INCIS achieving its technological aims, this hostility may have undermined the success of the system, as many other studies suggest.

In contrast, LINZ made a considerable and largely successful attempt to gain acceptance for the Landonline project from professional groups, and for their (literal) buy-in to the project. To an extent, the development was paid for by the users themselves, for example by setting aside surpluses generated by existing manual processes. While this excited a small degree of opposition, in general LINZ was successful in bringing on board professional associations for the development of the system. Indeed, LINZ was able to count on professional association support during 1999 when project termination was being advocated by Treasury. Similarly, the 2001 WAVE project and resulting report, which was the health sector's guiding information strategy until its replacement in mid-2005, was characterised by cross-sector representation and considerable consultation with all implicated parties. However, the 'buy-in' of users should not be overplayed. Even if professional associations were supportive of the Landonline development, this did not always translate into actual usage of the system by professionals.

Using Existing Technology and Limiting Scope Creep

INCIS was characterised by the use of undeveloped 'bleeding edge' technology, all of which ultimately failed. Specifications changed markedly during the development, in a process called 'scope creep'. Similarly, Health Waikato never clearly defined its IS needs. This, combined with a poorly constructed contract, meant there was a significant risk of scope creep within the SMS project. A supporting factor for the SMS purchase was the supposition that the system was 'tried and tested' in New Zealand at Capital Coast Health. However, SMS installation at Capital Coast Health was only just commencing at the time Health Waikato made its purchase. Thus, Capital Coast Health did not provide a working example of SMS, which, like INCIS, was ultimately abandoned. Subsequent monitoring regimes suggest a preference for existing technology and avoiding scope creep.

Landonline, despite the rhetoric of a 'world first development', proceeded on the presumption that it would use off-the-shelf technology as far as possible and attempted to use processes similar to those used elsewhere. LINZ was able to examine a number of similar and successful systems in operation. While there was some degree of technological uncertainty, reflected in the difficulty of actually designing and assembling many of the components, it was far from the 'leap in the dark' and the delusions of grandeur that characterised INCIS. Indeed, initial discussions of Landonline largely saw the development as simply automating existing processes, rather than the all-problems-of-the-world-will-be-solved rhetoric of INCIS. This was possibly a large part of its partial success.

Landonline was largely successful in limiting its scope. It had a reasonably simple and well-explained function of automating existing processes and did not try to be all things to all people. Once decided upon, technology was largely fixed. However, even with the use of available technology, the requirement that the technology's functionality be demonstrated, well-designed contracts, with tightly controlled and monitored developments, and payment contingent on performance, Landonline was still significantly over its initial budget and years late, with some doubt remaining about its financial benefits. For some time it was touch-and-go as to whether the project would be finished. It may be that Landonline is about as good as a large information system development can be in the public sector.

Conclusion: Pessimism and Public Sector ICT Development

If you want to increase the likelihood of computer project failure, we suggest you do the following:

(1) Have an extremely ambitious and expensive scope that demands the development of new and unproven technology and applications never achieved elsewhere. The grander the expectations and benefits projected for ICT, the better. The bigger the project, the more likely it will fail.

(2) Increase the complexity of this project by attempting organisational change along the lines of the latest management fad, and by linking this to the project. Continually change technical specifications during the development.

(3) Develop a long and complex contract, and assume this will solve any problems that might arise (and they will). Indeed, rather than divide the project up into contestable contracts, and divide hardware and software procurement, award the entire project to your favoured supplier without tendering.

(4) Rely on the advice and skills of contracted consultants, salespeople, and ICT suppliers, and do not develop your own capacity in ISD. Ensure a succession of different and competing consultants are involved, so institutional and overall project knowledge is fragmented.

(5) Have a project with a long timeframe of development to ensure technology is obsolete by the time the project is finished and that the risk of legislative change is increased.

(6) Believe everything you are told about progress of the development, whether it is from the developers, or internal or external monitoring, and assume that it will be 'right on the night'.

(7) Look for key indicators of forthcoming failure such as: misreporting of results, timetable slippages, the non-delivery of applications, budget overruns, personality clashes in the project development team and tensions with the intended users of the system. Do not decisively terminate the project in the face of these difficulties, however. Instead, reorganise management processes, monitoring regimes and so on along the lines of the newest management fad, and hire new managers and consultants, and add more programmers and technology, so you can assure everyone problems are being addressed.

(8) Continue to throw money at the project, as more and better technology or management improvements will surely deal with any problems, or at least prolong the project.

Only then will you have a full-blown fiasco on your hands.

What is particularly striking about the failures and partial success outlined in this book is the degree to which they repeat many of the same mistakes found in other ICT failures across the world and across decades of computer development. The degree of computer failure has not much changed during this time and most projects, particularly large projects, are unsuccessful. There is some evidence that monitoring and procurement regimes are improving in New Zealand, although they are sometimes ignored. But there seems little evidence that the New Zealand public sector has learned the key lessons of these failures: *large projects almost always fail*. Large projects continue to be initiated and government enthusiasm for ICT continues as the focus increasingly shifts to ambitious claims made for 'e-government'. As outlined in Chapter 2, governments in New Zealand and elsewhere have brought e-government to the centre of their policy agendas. Our model of the four enthusiasms of ICT failure:

- *idolisation* by public servants and politicians
- *lomanism* of IT companies and their employees
- *managerial faddism*
- *technophilia* of developers

suggests large projects will continue to be initiated, and will continue to fail. If so, doubt remains as to whether the goals of the e-government agenda will be achieved. If troubles and failure characterise large projects within individual departments and organisations, then less might be expected of e-government which depends on inter-agency IS development, and ultimately is a much larger project.

What then is to be done? Much of the writing on ICT failure suffers from what Oakeshott (1962) might term 'rationalism'; that is, a belief that there is some 'technique' that can be applied to IS developments that will fix them once and for all. However, that right technique – a new programming methodology, a new monitoring regime, a new management fad, a new consultancy template or whatever – has not been discovered yet; or if the right technique has been found, it has not yet been applied. This is why failure is still so common.

In the face of such optimism, and the four enthusiasms of ICT we have outlined, we suggest a degree of pessimism when it comes to IS development. This pessimism is based on a belief that the processes involved in IS developments are not fully understood, that their complexity makes them difficult if not impossible to control, and that large IS developments are likely to fail. IS developments in the public sector are not simply technical exercises in software engineering, the application of 'management science' and the talents of brilliant managers, or the bringing-in of highly skilled consultants – or even just some healthy combination of all of these. Rather, IS developments are a potent and complex mixture, amongst other things, of:

- dangerous enthusiasms
- unclear aims and technical specifications
- highly challenging technical problems
- the frailties of humans and management systems
- personality and other conflicts
- political infighting

- problems of agency and control
- legislative instability
- clashes of cultures between public servants, software developers, consultants, and salespersons and their respective organisations.

If one thing characterises large IS developments, it is this vast complexity. That these developments are often combined with other large-scale reorganisation, and technical and other specification changes are sometimes made during the development process, only compounds this complexity. We do not believe that, for the foreseeable future, some technique or techniques will ably manage this complexity. Indeed, as expectations about ICT and ISD continue to grow – most recently with the fashion for e-government – any improvements made in 'techniques' may be outpaced by the increasing demands of complexity on the all-too-human managers, public servants, software designers, and other members of the IS industry.

At its most basic level, pessimism raises the question whether new IS developments are actually of benefit. In the 'garbage can' of public management decision-making, the solution (which might be restructuring or investment in ICT or both) often exists quite separately from any identified problem (Cohen, March and Olsen 1972). If the first step, then, is to ask what is to be achieved and what problem is to be solved, the next question becomes: can this problem be solved without investment in further ICT? Can some minor adjustment to current systems of management or ICT deliver benefits without great costs and great disruption? Can some upgrade to present systems be carried out? If the costs, uncertainties, and risks of change and failure are great, do they potentially outweigh the inconveniences, costs, and difficulties of continuing with the status quo?

Does this pessimism – this expectation of failure – imply an abandonment of IS developments? In some cases, yes. Pessimism may have prevented INCIS being initiated and saved about $NZ100 million. This sum could have been spent more productively on upgrading police cars and buildings or 'fighting crime', or on a host of other pressing problems. The Police could have continued using the clunky and outdated Wanganui Computer for a few more years, possibly without great loss – which is what happened anyway. Across the globe, trillions of dollars have been poured away on public sector ICT developments for no benefit. Indeed, some systems have proven less effective than their predecessors. In many cases, if these vast sums had instead been spent on such prosaic things as schools, decent public transport and so on – and if the large IS projects had never been initiated – this would have been a good thing. This is dramatically underlined when a number of large IS failures have occurred in developing countries that are unable or unwilling to supply even the most basic public goods to their citizens (Heeks 2002).

If the decision is made to proceed with some ISD, then the question becomes how can this be done with the least disruption and the least cost, and with the least risk and uncertainty? The wrong answer would be to decide to invest in a high-risk, highly ambitious, large 'bleeding edge' development, with a long development timeframe, which has a very high probability of failure – such as INCIS. A more sensible solution might be to examine what is currently working in the market place and try to buy something off-the-shelf that can be demonstrated to work. However, it would not do to buy a system that did not fit the organisation's needs, and then adapt this system to particular legislative and organisational conditions. Once adaptations are attempted on an existing system, however well it might work in its home country or public sector, the probability of failure again becomes large – as the SMS failures at Health Waikato and Capital Coast Health show.

If the system does not exist anywhere else, then the question again should be: are the expectations held for ISD too high? If it is not possible to purchase a suitable off-the-shelf system, or one that approaches the organisation's 'needs', can expectations be scaled back to what does exist, or can the organisation get by without further ISD – at least until the technology improves? One of the key cautions that Police disregarded about the achievability of INCIS was the non-existence of a similar system elsewhere in the world. A few more years with an obsolete system is not going to be the end of the world. When the Police continued to use the Wanganui Computer, the sky did not fall in, nor did an explosion of crime occur: in fact, there was not much of a difference at all. The continued use by Health Waikato of the Hospro-W system, after the failure of the SMS project, had no perceivable impact on patient care and other outcomes. It is unlikely that the public sector is going to be competed out of existence by some 'first mover' in technology, even if this happens in the private sector. If the answer is still that an ISD is needed, then – and only then – should an ISD be considered.

Once the decision is made to proceed towards an ISD, pessimism should still be the guiding principle:

- Be modest about what can be achieved by ICT.
- Expect problems.
- Assume the promises and enthusiasms of internal and external IS people, salespeople, consultants, management gurus, technicians, and software engineers are probably not going to be worth much when a system fails – nor will any contract, even if it runs to thousands of pages.
- Believe that developments will work only when they can be shown to work. Developments that automate existing and routine processes are more likely to be successful.
- Be aware that long-term projects are more likely to be overtaken by legislative changes and by technology improvements and so be obsolete by the time they become operational.
- Realise that clashes of culture, problems of control, and the complexities of ISDs, make control and monitoring of projects extremely difficult.

- Accept that there is no reason to believe that the current or proposed ISDs can better avoid the problems that have plagued all other ISDs for decades, or that current managers and programmers, auditors and monitoring regimes are somehow superior to those that have failed in the past.
- If there is to be restructuring of the organisation, this should not be tied to the ISD, but carried out separately and beforehand.
- It is unwise to increase complexity by changing specifications during the development.
- Be prepared to terminate the development if cost overruns, delays, or non-delivery become apparent – despite claims it 'is almost there' or 'it will be right on the night'. The process of development may cause considerable and costly disruption of business that may never be recovered.
- The system, even if it does work, is unlikely to lead to huge job savings, or even cost savings in the short term – despite many projections and promises otherwise – and there may be a loss of productivity until staff become used to its idiosyncrasies.
- Excluding front-line staff from development is also a high-risk strategy, and they might undermine the system if it does work.

Above all, be pessimistic about information technology.

Notes

Chapter 1

1 New Public Management (often called 'managerialism') is a term applied to the host of writings and actions that seek to apply (assumed) and often idealised private sector management practices in the public sector. NPM sees management as a generic skill or technique that can be applied across all sectors, public and private. Influenced by economic models of behaviour that see humans as rationally optimising and opportunist individuals, and professional groups as largely vested or 'rent seeking' interests, NPM is suspicious of representative, democratic or deliberative types of decision-making. Rather, management and decision-making power should be centralised with the professional managers, who should be given greater autonomy – let managers manage – to achieve their objectives.

As humans are assumed to be opportunist and mainly motivated by pecuniary gain, NPM often focuses on short-term contracts and other financial controls to motivate and punish individuals. The faith shown in management as a skill is sometimes reflected in the adoption of management fads from the private sector, sometimes after they have ceased to be actually used in the private sector, and the use of private sector management and other consultants to advise and sometimes make decisions in public bodies. Reflecting the belief that the private sector is inherently more efficient, NPM advocates the attempted replication of market processes including the introduction of competition and quasi-markets, contracting-out and sometimes privatisation (Goldfinch 2004).

Chapter 3

1 HL7, or Health Level 7, is an agreed international standard for data exchange. See www.hl7.org.
2 Data and information may be either 'pushed' out to various implicated parties, for instance from District Health Boards to service providers, or available on a 'pull' or as requested basis.
3 Integrated care is a key aim of most advanced world health systems. Integration refers to closing the gaps between the various different locations and levels of service provided, for instance, between general practitioners and hospitals, between public and private services, and between different services in large organisations such as hospitals. Patients follow robust integration, patient records and funding, reducing the need for service duplication; and the patient experience with the health system is 'seamless'.
4 Enforcement of standards in health care settings is often difficult. For example, busy physicians in large and open hospital wards may be reluctant to log on each time they wish to use an information system, undermining system security.

Chapter 4

1 Crown Company Monitoring Advisory Unit was a division of the Treasury established in the early 1990s to protect the government's interests in Crown companies, including Crown Health Enterprises (public hospitals).

Chapter 5

1 This section draws heavily on the Sapphire Report (1994). This was prepared in August 1994 by the initial project team on the INCIS development for handover to the new project team.

2 Architecture in this sense is used to mean the overall design of a system, including the way different components of a system fit and work together.

3 Numbers differ in the Sapphire Report, where 160 organisations are said to have requested a copy, sixty-two organisations responded, and over twenty organisations requested to be considered for the role of prime contractor.

4 Inspector Tony Crewdson was appointed change manager in February 1994, then appointed INCIS project director in September 1994.

5 To rephrase this in terms of our model of enthusiasms (see Chapter 1), the lomanism of IBM fed into the idolisation of the Police in a vicious circle.

6 Net Present Value is a widely-used method of expressing the projected future benefits and costs of an investment in today's money. Future cash flows and benefits (which are assigned monetary values) and future costs (similarly assigned a monetary value) are 'discounted' back to the present day, usually by setting an interest rate or cost of capital (a 'discount rate'). The final figure is arrived at by subtracting the sum of discounted costs from the sum of discounted benefits.

7 Request for Proposal (RFP) and Request for Tender (RFT) are stages in the standard process when contracting for goods and services. The difference is that the response to an RFT requires a Tender with a firm proposal and costings.

8 The Small Report is contradictory on Crewdson's appointment – October on p. 44 and September on p. 218.

9 Doone claims that the report was further modified to take into account Batchelor's concerns and that the Andersen review of the project was also in response to these concerns. Batchelor had left the Police force by the time the report was delivered.

10 Small is contradictory seeing the resignation date of March on p. 50 and January on p. 218.

11 The new and untried (and ultimately unsuccessful) software technology of distributed OO client/server was replaced with a conventional three-tier client/server architecture, with INCIS applications to run on IBM's proprietary CICS (applications environment) and MVS (mainframe operating system) platform. The distributed client-server approach to large software systems is still a complicated and difficult design method to use. It requires the co-ordination of, potentially, hundreds of different software applications and databases on physically separate computers. Compare this with the centralised and well-tried three-tier approach, where a few large central servers (or frequently only one server) provide software applications to many small client computers. The three-tier client/server architecture was also used in the NIA, the successor to INCIS.

Chapter 6

1 It uses various PCs and Unix and Windows servers. It includes an Informix database, and Filenet is used as a server for indexing and the rendering of images. Citrix is used

for remote access. Geographic Information software from ESRI is used to manipulate the digital images of the title and survey data.

2   The Office of the Valuer-General was added in 1998.

3   Terralink was purchased by New Zealand Aerial Mapping and Dunedin's Animation Research for $7.2 million. In early 2002 it delivered eMap, which allowed online access to aerial photographs that gave detailed property information, including boundaries. Delivered before Landonline was finished, this was seen as a potential future competitor (Barton 2002).

4   The final figure paid out in penalty payments throughout the project was not released by LINZ, citing contractual obligations.

Chapter 7

1   Business Process Re-engineering is managerial jargon for changing how an organisation works by changing procedures, job descriptions, and organisational structure to perform a new business function or an existing function differently. BPR benefits are not altogether uncontested. Those of a suspicious mind might even suspect BPR is simply a new(ish) piece of managerial double-speak for job cuts, since one measurement used for BPR success is simply that headcounts have been reduced by 75 per cent. Indeed, it is possible that management and IS journals have left BPR behind and moved on to embrace yet other fads – such as 'knowledge management', or the 'learning organisation'.

References

Chapter 1

Abel-Hamid, T.K. 1988. Understanding the '90% Syndrome' in Software Project Management: A Simulation-Based Study. *The Journal of Systems and Software* 8 (4): 319–30.

Al-Gahtani, S.S., and M. King. 1999. Attitudes, satisfaction and usage: factors contributing to each in the acceptance of information technology. *Behaviour & Information Technology* 18 (4): 277–97.

Auditor-General of Canada. 2002. Report of the Auditor General of Canada to the House of Commons: Office of the Auditor-General.

Bascarini, D. 1999. The logical framework for defining project success. *Project Management Journal* 30 (4): 25–32.

Beetham, David. 1996. *Bureaucracy*. Second Edition, *Concepts in social thought*. Minneapolis: University of Minnesota Press.

Bell, Stephen. 2003. Govt orders independent review for legislation project. *Computerworld,* Wednesday 18 June.

Birnum, Robert. 2000. *Management Fads in Higher Education*. San Franciso: Jossey-Bass.

Bovens, Mark, and Paul 't Hart. 1996. *Understanding Policy Fiascos*. New Brunswick and London: Transaction Publishers.

Bovens, Mark, Paul 't Hart, and B. Guy Peters (eds) 2001. *Success and Failure in Public Governance*. Cheltenham: Edward Elgar.

Brimacombe, Phil. 2003. Health Care Information Systems: The Counties Manukau District Health Board Experience. In *Continuity Amid Chaos: Health Care Management and Delivery in New Zealand*, edited by R. Gauld. Dunedin: University of Otago Press.

Brindle, Margaret, and Peter N. Stearns. 2001. *Facing up to Management Faddism: A New Look at an Old Force*. Westport, CT: Quorum Books.

Bronson, Po. 1999. *The Nudist on the Late Shift and other Tales of Silicon Valley*. London: Vintage UK Random House.

Brown, M.M., and J. Brudney. 1998. Public sector information technology initiatives – Implications for programs of public administration. *Administration & society* 30 (4): 421–42.

Brown, M.M., and J.L. Brudney. 2003. Learning organizations in the public sector? A study of police agencies employing information and technology to advance knowledge. *Public Administration Review* 63(1): 30–43.

Bussen, Wendy, and Michael D. Myers. 1997. Executive information system failure: A New Zealand case study. *Journal of Information Technology* 12 (2): 145–53.

Cole, A. 1995. Runaway Projects: Cause and Effects. *Software World (UK)* 26 (3): 3–5.

Collins, Tony, and David Bicknell. 1997. *Crash, Ten Easy Ways to Avoid a Computer Disaster*. Simon & Schuster.

Coltman, Tim, Timothy M. Devinney, Alopi Latukefu, and David F. Midgley. 2001. E-business: revolution, evolution, or hype? *California Management Review* 44 (1): 57–86.

Corner, Ian, and Matthew Hinton. 2002. Customer relationship management systems: implementation risks and relationship dynamics. *Qualitative Market Research* 5 (4): 239–51.

Dalcher, Darren, and Audley Genus. 2003. Avoiding IS/IT Implementation Failure. *Technology Analysis and Strategic Management* 15 (4): 403–7.

Dale, Tony, and Shaun Goldfinch. 2002. *Pessimism as an Information System Management Tool in the Public Sector: Lessons from the INCIS Fiasco in the New Zealand Police Force*. Available from http://nz.cosc.canterbury.ac.nz/research/reports/TechReps/2002/tr_0202.pdf.

Dinsdale, Paul. 2004. Information Technology is not meeting nurses' needs: staff want to be involved in the development of the system they are expected to use. *Nursing Standard* 19 (7): 8–9.

du Gay, Paul. 2000. *In Praise of Bureaucracy: Weber, organization, ethics*. London: Sage.

Dutton, W.H., D. MacKenzie, S. Shapiro, and M. Peltu. 1995. Computer power and human limits: learning from IT and telecommunications disasters. *PICT Policy Research Paper No. 33*.

Economist, 2002. The health service's IT Problem. 19 October: 51–2.

Economist, 2004. Computerising the NHS: Deja Vu All Over Again? *Economist*, 14 October.

Evans, Mark and Reynolds, Chris. 2001. Software barely makes the grade. *Computerworld New Zealand*, 19 November 2001: 43.

Fenton, Norman and Pfleeger, Shari. 1997. *Software Metrics, A Rigorous & Practical Approach*. Second Edition ed. Boston, MA: PWS Publishing Company.

Georgiadou, E. 2003. Software Process and Product Improvement: A Historical Perspective. *Cybernetics and Systems Analysis* 39 (1): 125–42.

Ginzberg, M.J. 1981. Key recurrent issues in the MIS implementation process. *MIS Quarterly* 5 (2): 47–59.

Glass, R.L. 1998. Software Runaways – Some Surprising Findings. *The DATABASE for Advances in Information Systems* 28 (3): 16–19.

Glass, Robert. 1999. Evolving a New Theory of Project Success. *Communications of the ACM* 42 (11): 17–19.

Goldfinch, Shaun. 2004. Examining the National University Corporation Plan and University Reform in Japan. *The Journal of Finance and Management in Colleges and Universities* (1): 231–61.

Grant, Gerald. 2003. Strategic alignment and enterprise systems implementation: the case of Metalco. *Journal of Information Technology* 18 (3): 159–75.

Grover, V., Al Lederer, and R. Sabherwal. 1988. Recognizing the Politics of MIS. *Information & Management* 14 (3): 145–56.

Heeks, Richard (ed.) 1999. *Reinventing Government in the Information Age*. London: Routledge.

Heeks, Richard. 2002. *Failure, Success and Improvisation of Information System Projects in Developing Countries*. Manchester: Institute for Development Policy and Management.

Heeks, Richard, D. Mundy, and A. Salazar. 1999. Why Health Care Information Systems Succeed or Fail. In *Information Systems for Public Sector Management: Working Paper Series, paper no. 9*. Manchester: Institute for Development Policy and Management: Manchester University.

Heeks, Richard, and Subhash Bhatnagar. 1999. Understanding success and failure in information age reform. In R. Heeks (ed.), *Reinventing Government in the Information Age*. London and New York: Routledge.

Hewson, N., and W. Hewson. 1998. *ROI in sales and marketing systems*. Cambridge: Hewson Consulting Group.

Holden, Stephen. 2003. The Evolution of Information Technology Management at the Federal Level: Implications for Public Administration. In G.D. Garson Hershey (ed.), *Public Information Technology: Policy and Management Issues*. London, Melbourne: Idea Group Publishing.

Huang, Jimmy, Enesi Makoju, Sue Newel, and Robert Galliers. 2003. Opportunities to learn from 'failure' with electronic commerce: a case study of electronic banking. *Journal of Information Technology* 18 (1): 17–26.

Iacovou, Charalambous. 1999. The IPACS Project: when IT hits the fan. *Journal of Information Technology* 14 (2): 267–75.

Irani, Z., A.M. Sharif, and P.E.D. Love. 2001. Transforming failure into success through organisational learning: an analysis of a manufacturing information system. *European Journal of Information Systems* 10 (1): 55–66.

Jacobson, Ivar, James Rumbaugh, and Grady Booch. 1998. *The Unified Software Development Process, Object Technology*. Addison Wesley Longman Inc.

James, G. 1997. IT fiascos and how to avoid them. *Datamation* November: 84–8.

Keil, Mark, Joan Mann, and Arun Rai. 2000. Why software projects escalate: An empirical analysis and test of four theoretical models. *MIS Quarterly* 24 (4): 631–64.

Keil, Mark, and Daniel Robey. 2001. Blowing the Whistle on Troubled Software Projects. *Communications of the ACM* 44 (4): 87–93.

Knights, David, and Fergus Murray. 1994. *Managers divided: organisation politics and information technology management, Wiley series in information systems*. Chichester [England]; New York: J. Wiley.

Korac-Boisvert, N., and A. Kouzmin. 1995. Transcending soft-core IT disasters in public sector organizations. *Information Infrastructure and Policy* 4 (2): 131–61.

Kwon, T.H., and R.W. Zmud. 1987. Unifying the fragmented models of information systems implementation. In R.J. Bolland and R.A. Hirscheim (eds), *Critical Issues in Information Systems Research*. New York: Wiley.

Larsen, M.A., and M.D. Myers. 1999. When success turns into failure: a package-driven business process re-engineering project in the financial services industry. *Journal of Strategic Information Systems* 8 (4): 395–417.

Laudon, Kenneth. C., and Jane. P. Laudon. 1998. *Management Information Systems: New Approaches Organisation and Technology*. Englewood Cliffs, New Jersey: Prentice-Hall.

Lindblom, C. 1988[1959]. The 'Science' of Muddling Through. In *Democracy and Market System*. New York and London: Norwegian University Press.

Lucas, H. 1981. *Implementation: the key to successful information systems*. New York: Columbia University Press.

Lyytinen, Kalle, and Daniel Robey. 1999. Learning failure in information systems development. *Information Systems Journal* 9 (2): 85–101.

Mahaney, Robert, and Albert Lederer. 1999. Runaway Information System Projects and Escalating Commitment. *SIGCPR '99*: 291–6.

March, James G., and Johan P. Olsen. 1996. Institutional Perspectives on Political Institutions. *Governance* 9 (3): 247–64.

Merton, R.K. 1957. *Social Theory and Social Structure*. New York: Free Press.

Milne, Jonathan. 2002. Department "not working at all well". *The Dominion*, 4 March 2002: 2.

Nandhakumar, J. 1996. Design–for success? Critical success factors in executive information systems development. *European Journal of Information Systems* 5 (1): 62–72.

Norris, Donald F., and M. Jae Moon. 2005. Advancing E-Government at the Grassroots: Tortoise or Hare? *Public Administration Review* 65 (1): 64–75.

Northrop, Alana, Kenneth Kraemer, Debora Dunkle, and John King. 1990. Payoffs from Computerization – Lessons over Time. *Public Administration Review* 50 (5): 505–14.

Popper, Micha, and Raanan Lipshitz. 2000. Organizational learning – Mechanisms, culture, and feasibility. *Management Learning* 31 (2): 181–96.

Rocheleau, Bruce. 2003. Politics, Accountability, and Governmental Information Systems. In *Public Information Technology: Policy and Management Issues*, G.D. Garson (ed.). Hershey, London, Melbourne: Idea Group Publishing.

Royal Academy of Engineering and British Computer Society. 2004. *The Challenges of Complex IT Projects*. London: The Royal Academy of Engineering.

Salaman, Graeme. 2001. A response to Snell. The learning Organisation: Fact or Fiction? *Human Relations* 54 (3): 319–42.

SIMPL/NZIER. 2000. Information technology projects: Performance of the New Zealand public sector in performance. Report to the Department of the Prime Minister and Cabinet. Wellington: The SIMPL Group and New Zealand Institute of Economic Research (INC).

Small, Francis. 2000. Ministerial Inquiry into INCIS. Wellington.

Smith, H. Jeff, Mark Keil, and Gordon Depledge. 2001. Keeping mum as the project goes under: Toward an explanatory model. *Journal of Management Information Systems* 18 (2): 189–227.

Standish Group. 2001. *Extreme Chaos*. Available from http://www.standishgroup.com/sample_research/PDFpages/extreme_chaos.pdf.

Standish Group. 2004. *Third quarter Report 2004*. Available from http://www.standishgroup.com/sample_research/PDFpages/q3-spotlight.pdf.

Swanson, E.B. 1988. *Information System Implementation: Bridging the Gap between Designing and Implementation*. Henley-on-Thames: Alfred Waller.

't Hart, Paul. 1994. *Groupthink in Government: A Study of Small Groups and Policy Failure*. Baltimore: John Hopkins UP.

Teega Associates Ltd. 2003. *Automation Program Evaluation*. Wellington: LINZ.

Tesser, A., and S. Rosen. 1972. Fear of negative evaluation and the reluctance to transmit bad news. *Journal of Communication* 22 (2): 124–41.

Turner, Ian. *Strategy, Complexity and Uncertainty*. 1998. Available from http://www.poolonline.com/archive/iss1fea5.html.

Wastell, David G. 1999. Learning dysfunctions in information systems development: Overcoming the social defences with transitional objects. *MIS Quarterly* 23 (4): 581–600.

Wilcocks, Leslie. 1994. Managing information systems in UK public administration: issues and prospects. *Public Administration* 72 (1): 13–32.

Wilson, M., and D. Howcroft. 2002. Reconceptualising failure: social shaping meets IS research. *European Journal of Information Systems* 11: 236–50.

Chapter 2

6, Perri, Diana Leat, Kimberly Seltzer, and Gerry Stoker. 2002. *Towards Holistic Governance: The New Reform Agenda*. Houndmills: Palgrave.

Australian National Audit Office. 2005. *Measuring the Efficiency and Effectiveness of E-Government*. Canberra: Australian National Audit Office.

Blair, Tony. 2005. *Prime Minister's Mission for E-Government Unit*. London: Cabinet Office. Available from http://www.cabinetoffice.gov.uk/e-government/.

Boston, Jonathan, John Martin, June Pallot, and Pat Walsh. 1996. *Public Management: The New Zealand Model*. Auckland: Oxford University Press.

Brown, Gordon. 2004. *Statement by the Chancellor of the Exchequer on the 2004 Spending Review, 12 July*. London: HM Treasury, Chancellor of the Exchequer.

Bush, George W. 2002. *The Importance of E-Government. Presidential Memo*. Washington D.C.: Office of the President of the United States. Available from http://www.whitehouse.gov/omb/egov/g-1-background.html.

Cabinet Office. 1998. *Our Information Age: The Government's Vision*. London: Cabinet Office.

Cabinet Office. 1999. *Modernising Government*. London: Cabinet Office.

Cabinet Office. 2000. *E-Government: A Strategic Framework for Government*. London: Cabinet Office.

Cabinet Office. 2004. *Autumn Performance Report 2004*. London: Cabinet Office.

Central Information Technology Unit. 1996. *Government Direct: A Prospectus for the Electronic Delivery of Government Services*. London: Central Information Technology Unit/Office of Public Service.

Chadwick, A., and C. May. 2003. Interaction Between States and Citizens in the Age of the Internet: 'E-government' in the United States, Britain and the European Union. *Governance* 16 (2): 271–300.

Commonwealth Fund. 2005. Frist, Clinton Pledge Health Care IT Push. *The Commonwealth Fund: Washington Health Policy Week in Review,* 16 June.

Dugdale, Anni, Anne Daly, Franco Papandrea, and Maria Maley. 2005. Accessing E-government: Challenges for Citizens and Organizations. *International Review of Administrative Sciences* 71 (1): 109–118.

European E-Government Observatory. 2004. *New Head of UK E-Government Outlines Key Priorities*. European Union. Available from http://europa.eu.int/idabc/en/document/3271/345.

Evening Post, The. 1999. Editorial. *The Evening Post*, 28 October: 4.

Fountain, Jane. 2001. *Building the Virtual State: Information Technology and Institutional Change*. Washington DC: Brookings Institute Press.

Halligan, John, and Trevor Moore. 2004. *Future Challenges for E-Government*. Canberra: Australian Government Information Management Office & Institute of Public Administration Australia ACT Division.

Ho, A.T.K. 2002. Reinventing Local Governments and the E-government Initiative. *Public Administration Review* 64 (2): 434–44.

Holliday, Ian. 2001. Steering the British State in the Information Age. *Government and Opposition* 36 (3): 314–29.

Hudson, John. 2002. Digitising the Structures of Government: The UK's Information Age Government Agenda. *Policy and Politics* 30 (4): 515–31.

International Telecommunication Union. 2004. *Economies by Broadband Penetration.* Available from http://www.itu.int/ITU-D/ict/statistics/at_glance/top20_broad_2004. html, 2005.

Layne, K, and J Lee. 2001. Developing Fully Functional E-Government: A Four Stage Model. *Government Information Quarterly* 18: 122–36.

Mahrer, Harald, and Robert Krimmer. 2005. Towards the Enhancement of E-democracy: Identifying the Notion of the 'Middleman Paradox'. *Information Systems Journal* 15 (1): 27–42.

Mallard, Trevor. 2001a. *New Zealand E-Government Strategy – April 2001.* Wellington: Minister of State Services.

Mallard, Trevor. 2001b. *New Zealand E-Government Strategy – December 2001 – Update.* Wellington: Minister of State Services.

Mallard, Trevor. 2003. *New Zealand E-Government Strategy – June 2003 – Update.* Wellington: Minister of State Services.

Mallard, Trevor, and Michael Cullen. 2001. *Report of the Advisory Group on the Review of the Centre.* Wellington: State Services Commission.

Ministry of Economic Development. 2005. *Digital Strategy: A Draft New Zealand Digital Strategy for Consultation.* Wellington: Ministry of Economic Development.

National Office for the Information Economy. 1998. *Strategic Framework for the Information Economy.* Canberra: National Office for the Information Economy.

National Office for the Information Economy. 2000. *Government Online. The Commonwealth Government's Strategy. April 2000.* Canberra: National Office for the Information Economy.

National Office for the Information Economy. 2002. *Better Services, Better Government.* Canberra: National Office for the Information Economy.

Norris, Pippa. 2001. *Digital Divide: Civic Engagement, Information Poverty, and the Internet Worldwide.* Cambridge: Cambridge University Press.

Norris, Pippa. 2003. *Deepening Democracy via E-governance. Draft paper for the UN.* World Public Sector Report. Available from: www.pippanorris.com.

Office of Management and Budget. 2004. *Expanding E-Government: Partnering for a Results-Oriented Government, December 2004.* Washington DC: Executive Office of the President, Office of Management and Budget.

Point Topic. 2005. *World Broadband Statistics to Q1 05.* Available from http://www.point-topic.com/default.asp.

Police. National Strategy for Police Information and Technology Systems 2001-4. 20 April 2001. Available from http://www.police.govt.nz/Police_it_strategy.pdf.

Pollitt, Christopher. 2003. Joined-Up Government: A Survey. *Political Studies Review* 1: 34–49.

Reddick, Christopher G. 2005. Citizen Interaction with E-Government: From the Streets to Servers? *Government Information Quarterly* 22 (1): 38–57.

Self, Peter. 1993. *Government by the Market? The Politics of Public Choice.* Boulder: Westview Press.

Silcock, R. 2001. What is E-Government? *Parliamentary Affairs* 54: 88–101.

State Services Commission. 2004. *Achieving E-Government 2004: A Report on Progress Towards the New Zealand E-Government Strategy.* Wellington: State Services Commission.

State Services Commission. 2005. *Development Goals for the State Services.* Wellington: State Services Commission.

Steering Group Managing for Outcomes. 2002. *Managing for Outcomes: Guidance for Departments*. Wellington: State Services Commission.

Thomas, John Clayton, and G. Streib. 2003. The New Face of Government: Citizen-initiated Contacts in the Era of E-government. *Journal of Public Administration Research and Theory* 13 (1): 83–101.

Thomas, John Clayton, and Gregory Streib. 2005. E-democracy, E-commerce and E-research: Examining the Electronic Ties Between Citizens and Government. *Administration and Society* 37 (3): 259–80.

Torres, Lourdes, Vicente Pina, and Basilio Acerete. 2005. E-Government Developments on Delivering Public Services Among EU Cities. *Government Information Quarterly* 22 (2): 217–38.

United Nations Public Administration Network. 2004. *UN Global E-Government Readiness Report 2004*. New York: United Nations.

Walsh, Kieron. 1995. *Public Services and Market Mechanisms: Competition, Contracting and the New Public Management*. London: Macmillan.

Wicklund, Hans. 2005. A Habermasian Analysis of the Deliberative Democratic Potential of ICT-Enabled Services in Swedish Municipalities. *New Media and Society* 7 (2): 247–70.

Chapter 3

Bolger, J.B., R. Richardson, and W.F. Birch. 1990. *Economic and Social Initiative – December 1990. Statements to the House of Representatives*. Wellington: Government Print.

Boston, Jonathan, and Paul Dalziel (eds) 1992. *The Decent Society: Essays in Response to National's Economic and Social Policies*. Auckland: Oxford University Press.

Brimacombe, Phil. 2003. Health Care Information Systems: The Counties Manukau District Health Board Experience. In *Continuity Amid Chaos: Health Care Management and Delivery in New Zealand*, R. Gauld (ed.). Dunedin: University of Otago Press.

Casilino, L., R.R. Gillies, S.M. Shortell, *et al.* 2003. External incentives, information technology, and organized processes to improve health care quality for patients with chronic diseases. *Journal of the American Medical Association* 289 (4): 434–41.

Cumming, J., and N. Mays. 2002. How sustainable is New Zealand's latest health system restructuring? *Journal of Health Services Research and Policy* 7 (Suppl. 1): 46–55.

Gauld, Robin. 2001. *Revolving Doors: New Zealand's Health Reforms*. Wellington: Institute of Policy Studies and Health Services Research Centre.

Gauld, Robin (ed.) 2003. *Continuity amid Chaos: Health Care Management and Delivery in New Zealand*. Dunedin: University of Otago Press.

Gibbs, A., D. Fraser, and J. Scott. 1988. Unshackling the Hospitals: Report of the Hospital and Related Services Taskforce. Wellington: Hospital and Related Services Taskforce.

Health Funding Authority. 1999. Health Funding Authority Strategic Plan for Information and Technology Management. Wellington: Health Funding Authority.

Health Funding Authority and Ministry of Health. 2000. Riding the Wave: Health Information Priorities. Wellington: Health Funding Authority and Ministry of Health.

Health Information Strategy Steering Committee. 2005. *Health Information Strategy for New Zealand*. Wellington: Ministry of Health.

Jack, M., L. Malcolm, P. Maxwell, and P. Finlay. 1990. *Developing a National Health Information System*. Wellington: Department of Health.

King, Annette. 2001. *The New Zealand Health Strategy.* Wellington: Ministry of Health.

King, Annette. 2001a. *The Primary Health Strategy*. Wellington: Ministry of Health.

Love, Tom. 2003. Continuing Change in Primary Care: Issues for Independent Practitioner Associations and Primary Health Organisations. In R. Gauld (ed.), *Continuity Amid Chaos: Health Care Management and Delivery in New Zealand*. Dunedin: University of Otago Press.

Ministry of Health. 2002. *Doing Better for New Zealanders: Better Health, Better Participation, Reduced Inequalities: Advice to the Incoming Minister of Health*. Wellington: Ministry of Health.

New Zealand Health Information Service. 1993. Issues in Developing and Implementing a Health Information System. Wellington: New Zealand Health Information Service.

Rowe, Ian, and Phil Brimacombe. 2003. Integrated care information technology. *New Zealand Medical Journal* 116 (1169).

Scott, C., G. Fougere, and J. Marwick. 1986. Choices for Health Care: Report of the Health Benefits Review. Wellington: Health Benefits Review.

Shipley, J. 1995. Advancing Health in New Zealand. Wellington: Ministry of Health.

Shipley, J. 1996. Health Information Strategy for the Year 2000. Wellington: Ministry of Health.

Systems Architecture Project Team. 2001. Systems Architecture: Current State Analysis. Unpublished report to the WAVE Board, Wellington.

Upton, Simon. 1991. *Your Health and the Public Health: A Statement of Government Health Policy*. Wellington: Government Print.

WAVE Advisory Board. 2001. From Strategy to Reality: The WAVE Project. Wellington: Ministry of Health.

WAVE Organisation Design Project. 2001. Organisation Design: Working Paper. Memorandum for Board Meeting of 24 May 2001, Wellington.

Williamson, M. 1991. Health Information Strategy for New Zealand: A Joint Venture Between the Area Health Boards and the Department of Health. Wellington: Department of Health.

Chapter 4

Anderson, Steve. 1998. Re: Computer Systems, 12 November. Wellington: CCMAU.

Association of Salaried Medical Specialists. 2003. Doctors Get No Joy in Saying 'We Told You So'. *Scoop.co.nz*, 20 October.

Audit New Zealand. 1999. Health Waikato Ltd, 19 August. Wellington: Audit New Zealand.

Bell Gully. 1999. Health Waikato Ltd: IT Systems Purchase Review. Report 6 December. Auckland: Bell Gully.

Bunkle, Phillida. 1998. Questions Over Ten Million Dollar Computer System, 27 November.

CCMAU – *see* Crown Company Monitoring Advisory Unit.

Chapman Tripp. 1999. SMS Agreement, 26 October. Auckland: Chapman Tripp.

Controller and Auditor-General. 1999. Capital Coast Health Ltd: New Computerised Information System. Report of the Controller and Auditor-General. Fourth Report of 1999. Wellington: Controller and Auditor-General.

Crown Company Monitoring Advisory Unit. 1998a. Health Waikato Ltd – 10 December. Wellington: CCMAU.

Crown Company Monitoring Advisory Unit. 1998b. Health Waikato Ltd – 30 November. Wellington: CCMAU.

Crown Company Monitoring Advisory Unit. 1999. Health Waikato Ltd: Resignation of Deputy Chair. Wellington: CCMAU.

Crown Company Monitoring Advisory Unit. 2000. Health Waikato Ltd – SMS IT System. Report to Ministers of Health and Finance. Wellington: CCMAU.

Deloitte and Touche Consulting Ltd. 1997. Health Waikato Ltd: Comparison of SMS and Hospro-W Implementation Options.

Gardner, Teresa. 1998. Hospital's Computer Pick Has Staff Angry. *The New Zealand Herald*, 27 November.

Gauld, Robin. 2000. Big Bang and the Policy Prescription: Health Care Meets the Market in New Zealand. *Journal of Health Politics, Policy and Law* 25 (5): 815–44.

Guysan, Claire. 2000. CCH Computer Obsolete, King Says. *The Evening Post*, 3 May: 3.

Health Waikato Ltd. 1997a. Clinical Information Systems Plan. Hamilton: Health Waikato Ltd.

Health Waikato Ltd. 1997b. Info 2000+ Project Report. Hamilton: Health Waikato Ltd.

Health Waikato Ltd. 1997c. Information Systems 1997–2000: The Way Ahead. Hamilton: Health Waikato Ltd.

Health Waikato Ltd. 1997d. Information Systems Strategy: An Opportunity for Redirection. Hamilton: Health Waikato Ltd.

Health Waikato Ltd. 1997e. Terms of Reference: Info 2000+. Hamilton: Health Waikato Ltd.

Health Waikato Ltd. 1998a. Information Systems. Hamilton: Health Waikato Ltd.

Health Waikato Ltd. 1998b. Information Systems – Future Direction. A report prepared for the Health Waikato Board of Directors by the Acting Chief Executive. Hamilton: Health Waikato Ltd.

Health Waikato Ltd. 1998c. Information Systems Strategic Partner Selection Report. Hamilton: Health Waikato Ltd.

Health Waikato Ltd. 1998d. Media Release, 26 November. Hamilton: Health Waikato Ltd.

Health Waikato Ltd. 1999a. Chronicle of Events: Information Systems. Hamilton: Health Waikato Ltd.

Health Waikato Ltd. 1999b. Health Waikato: Information System Purchase. Hamilton: Health Waikato Ltd.

Health Waikato Ltd. 1999c. Terms of Reference for IT System Acquisition Process Assurance Review. Hamilton: Health Waikato Ltd.

Health Waikato Ltd. 2000. HWL Response to the Seranova Report. Hamilton: Health Waikato Ltd.

Health Waikato Ltd Board. 1998. Board Meeting Minutes. Item 8: Information Systems – Future Direction, 24 November. Hamilton: Health Waikato Ltd.

Health Waikato Ltd Board. 1999. Submission by Health Waikato Ltd Board on Consultation Draft, October 1999. Hamilton: Health Waikato Ltd.

Howard, Karen. 1998. Controversial Computer System for Waikato. *The Dominion*, 28 November: 3.

Hunter Group. 1997. Report Proposing a Strategic Process for Selecting a PMS/CIS.

Jackson, Ivan, and David Keane. 1999. Capital Coast Health Ltd: Acquiring and Implementing Integrated Information Systems. Wellington: School of Communications and Information Management.

Jenkins, Jack. 1998. Letter to Steve Anderson, Principal Advisor – Health, Crown Company Monitoring Advisory Unit, 18 December. Hamilton.

Jenkins, Jack. n.d. Summary of Chair's Description of Process Followed by HWL for IT System Acquisition. Hamilton.

King, Annette. 2000. Millions of Health Dollars Wasted. Media Release, Office of the Minister of Health, 2 May.

Lamb, Max. 1999. Letter to Jack Jenkins. 18 January. Hamilton.

MacDonald, Nikki. 2004. More Delays for Health Board's IT Project. *The Dominion Post*, 27 November: 8.

Mold, Francesca. 1998. Hospital Buys $10 Million System. *The Waikato Times*, 26 November: 1.

Mold, Francesca. 1999. Health Boss Left with Hush Money. *The Waikato Times*, 19 June: 1.

New Zealand Press Association. 1999a. Computer Woes. *New Zealand Herald*, 23 April.

New Zealand Press Association. 1999b. Health Boss Quits Early. *The New Zealand Herald*, 20 December: A6.

New Zealand Press Association. 1999c. Health Waikato Computer Purchase to be Reviewed. *The Waikato Times*, 3 February.

New Zealand Press Association. 1999d. Hospital's $26m Computer System Can't Do Job – Staff. *The Evening Post*, 22 April: 1.

New Zealand Press Association. 2000a. Ditched System Bill May Be $18 million. *The Waikato Times*, 3 May: 1.

New Zealand Press Association. 2000b. Former Chairman Defends Decision. *The Waikato Times*, 2 May.

New Zealand Press Association. 2000c. Heads Roll After $9m Wasted on IT System. *Otago Daily Times*, 3 May: 14.

North, Rosemarie. 2000. Computer System Ditched. *The Waikato Times*, 2 May: 1.

Optimation New Zealand. 1998. Proposed Technologies Review for Health Waikato Ltd.

Pepperell, Susan. 2000. Terminal Illness: How $11 Million of Public Money was Wasted at Waikato Hospital. *Waikato Times*, 3 June: 13–14.

Seranova. 2000. Independent Review of Infolinks Project Report, 12 April.

Shipley, J. 1995. Advancing Health in New Zealand. Wellington: Ministry of Health.

Shipley, J. 1996. Health Information Strategy for the Year 2000. Wellington: Ministry of Health.

Simsion Bowles and Associates. 1999. Infolinks Project Review: SMS Application Functionality and Scope Assessment. Draft. 14 December.

Simsion Bowles and Associates. 2000a. Health Waikato: Infolinks: Options. 6 February.

Simsion Bowles and Associates. 2000b. Infolinks Project Review. Infolinks Options, Analysis and Recommendations. 7 April.

Weeks, Andrew. 1998. Letter to Jack Jenkins. Re: Information Technology Strategy. 13 November. Wellington: CCMAU.

White, Jan. 1999. Letter to Chris Russell, CCMAU. Re: Assurance Review of IT System Acquisition – Health Waikato. 3 August. Hamilton: Health Waikato Ltd.

Chapter 5

Bell, Stephen. 1999. Police chairman admits INCIS makes no difference to coppers on the beat. *The Independent*, 9 June 1999: 24.

Beynen, Martin van. 1999. Legal battle looms over INCIS affair. *The Press*, 10 August: 1.

Birch, W.F. 1999. Memorandum for Cabinet. INCIS Negotiating Strategy. SSC archive L-3–21/6.

Brown, Russell. 1999. 175 jobs to go along with INCIS. *Computerworld NZ*, 10 August 1999. Chamberlain, Jenny. 1997. NZPD Blues: Can Cops Cope? *North and South*, October 1997, 34–43.

Crewdson, A.J. 1995. INCIS Project Status Report: SSC archive L-3–21/5.

Crewsdon, A.J. 1996. Status Report.

Ernst and Young. 1993. Report on Review of INCIS Project. Obtained under the Official Information Act 1982.

Evening Post, The. 1999. Editorial. *The Evening Post*. 28 October: 4.

Finance, Minister of, Minister of Police, and Associate Treasurer. 1998. Minute re 1998 Police Budget. SSC archive L-3–21/16.

Fisk, C. 1993. Treasury InterOffice memo from Clement Fisk to Michael Moriarty Quality of Police Financial Management. SSC archive L-3–21/13.

Hawkins, George. 2001. $13.2 (ex GST) Million Police Vehicle Package Announced: Ministerial Press Release.

Hawkins, George. 2001. $60 million to address years of property neglect: Ministerial press release.

Jackson, Randal. 1998. *INCIS: Has it had a bum rap? Randal Jackson interviews Tony Crewdson* IDG98. 18 April. Available from http://www.idg.net.nz/.

Mallard, Trevor. 2000. Government to sell INCIS mainframe: Ministerial Press Release.

Matthews, B. 1996. Letter to the Office Solicitor of the SSC, D J Bradshaw. SSC archive L-3–21/14.

Matthews, B. 1998. Fax to Brendan Kelly (SSC). Re INCIS Cabinet Paper. SSC archive L-3–21/19.

Matthews, B. 1999. INCIS Status Report to the end of December 1998. SSC archive L-3–21/39.

NZ Police 2001. *National Strategy for Police Information and Technology Systems 2001–4*. 20 April 2001. Available from http://www.police.govt.nz/Policeitstrategy.pdf.

NZ Police. 2004. Annual Report. Wellington: NZ Police.

Pamatatau, Richard. 2001. Police brief companies on building "Incis 2". *NZ Infotech Weekly*, 17 April 2001: 1.

Press, The. 2000. Discord led to INCIS bungle, says report. *The Press*, 18 November 2000: 3.

Price Waterhouse. 1997. NZ Police INCIS Project Internal Audit. Price Waterhouse.

Provost, Lyn. 1998. INCIS Project – Options for strengthening. SSC archive L-3–21/18.

Rapley, J. 1997. SSC Memorandum re Police INCIS project – risks. SSC archive L-3–21/17.

Sapphire. 1994. Sapphire Technology Ltd. Report on INCIS.

Secretary for the Treasury. 1997. Letter from the Secretary for the Treasury to the Treasurer and the Minister of Finance. T97C/502. SSC archive L-3–21/7.

Shennan, M. 1999. INCIS: Response to Andersen Consulting Advice. Treasury document GD/33/6/1. SSC archive L-3–21/23.

Small, Francis. 2000. Ministerial Inquiry into INCIS. Wellington.

Soar, Jeffrey. 1999. Letter to Peter Doone re Gibralter Review of Police I and T Costs. SSC archive L-3–21/20.

Treasury, The. 1997. Letter from the Secretary for the Treasury to Police Commissioner Peter Doone, Treasury document GD/33/0. SSC archive L-3–21/17.

Waitai, Rana. 1999. Inquiry into CARD and INCIS. Justice and Law Reform Committee.

Williamson, Hon. Maurice. 1993. Meeting between Hon. Maurice Williamson and Police Commissioner re: the new Police Computer System INSYS. 15 September.

Williamson, M. 1994. Letter to the Minister of Police, Hon John Luxton, re: "Integrated National Crime Investigation System (INCIS)". SSC archive L-3–21/20.

Chapter 6

Audit Office. 2003. 2002/03 Financial Review. Audit Office Briefing to the Primary Reduction Committee. Wellington: LINZ.

Ballard, R. 1997. Land Information New Zealand: Titles and Survey Automation. Wellington: Chair Officials Committee on Expenditure Control.

Ballard, R. 2000. Land Information New Zealand: Information Technology: Survey and Titles Automation. Progress Report for the Month Ending February 2000. Wellington.

Ballard, Russ. 1997. Internal Memo. Cabinet Gives Automation Greenlight. Wellington: LINZ.

Ballard, Russ. 1999. Report to the Ministerial Subcommittee on the Land Information New Zealand (LINZ) Survey and Title Automation Program. Wellington: LINZ.

Ballard, Russ. 2000a. Land Information New Zealand: Information Technology Development: Survey and Title IS Automation (Landonline). Progress Report for June 2000. Wellington: LINZ.

Ballard, Russ. 2000b. Land Information New Zealand: Information Technology Development: Survey and Titles Automation (Landonline). Progress Report for July 2000. Wellington: LINZ.

Barton, Chris. 2002. Property details available on new website. *The New Zealand Herald*, 12 February.

Buddle Finlay. 1999. Survey and Land Title Automation Program ('Landonline Project RAM') – Peer Review of LINZ Contracts. Buddle Finlay.

Cabinet. 1999. Cabinet CAB (99) M 15/7. Wellington: Cabinet Office.

Cabinet Strategy Subcommittee on Expenditure Control and Government Administration (CSSECGA). 1999. Land Information New Zealand: Information Technology Development: Survey and Titles Automation. Wellington: Cabinet Strategy Subcommittee on Expenditure Control and Government Administration.

Dominion, The. 1999a. Linz denies unfair play in EDS tender. *The Dominion*, 16 August: 5.

Dominion, The. 1999b. Linz seeks more money to complete Landonline. *The Dominion*, 17 May: 1.

Dominion, The. 2000a. Land Information splits Landonline project. *The Dominion*, 27 March: 4.

Dominion, The. 2000b. Landonline tenders called for. *The Dominion*, 17 January: 2.

Dominion, The. 2000c. Linz blames $46.5m blow-out on forecasting. *The Dominion*, 24 March 2.

Dominion, The. 2000d. World first. *The Dominion*, 28 August: 10.

Dominion, The. 2001. Bytes. *The Dominion*, 17 April: 4.

Dominion, The. 2002. 25 staff added to fix LINZ systems. *The Dominion*, 6 February: 2.

Dominion Post, The. 2004. Computer system a success. *The Dominion Post*, 17 May: 10.

Espiner, Colin. 2000. Tighter rein by Govt on Landonline. *The Press*, 3 April: 9.

Evening Post, The. 1999. Treasury cease blowouts on IT projects, papers show. *The Evening Post*: 2.

Howie, Craig. 2002. Computer glitches wreck property deals. *The Dominion*, 15 February: 1.

LINZ. 2004. Written Response to Questions.

Luxton, John. 1999. Land Information New Zealand: Information Technology Development: Survey and Titles Automation. Wellington: Office of the Minister for Food, Fibre, Biosecurity and Border Control.

Mallard, Trevor. 2000. Land Information New Zealand: information technology development: survey and title IS automation (Landonline): Progress Report. Wellington: Office of the Minister for Land Information.

Office of the Minister of Lands. 1997. Business Case: Land Information New Zealand: Information Technology Development: Survey and Land Titles Automation: Office of the Minister of Lands. Obtained under the Official Information Act 1982.

Opticon. 2002. *Landonline Project*. QA Report 10/01. Melbourne: Opticon.

Opticon Australia. 2000. QA Review 06/00 Landonline project. Opticon Australia.

Price Waterhouse Urwick. 1997. Land Information New Zealand. External Benefits Quantification. Final Report. Price Waterhouse Urwick.

Primary Production Committee. 2003. Final Transcript. Primary Production Committee Financial Review. Wellington: NZ House of Representatives.

Primary Production Committee. 2005. Report of the Primary Production Committee. 2005/06 Estimates: Vote Lands. Wellington: NZ House of Representatives.

Pullar-Strecker, Tom. 1999a. Landonline software ready to test. *The Dominion*, 18 October: 7.

Pullar-Strecker, Tom. 1999b. Money short as LINZ project strikes snag. *The Dominion*, 1 February: 2.

Pullar-Strecker, Tom. 2000. Landonline hits trouble in Dunedin. *The Dominion*, 31 July: 1.

Pullar-Strecker, Tom. 2001. Report criticised Landonline. *The Dominion*, 20 August: 1.

Pullar-Strecker, Tom. 2002. Landonline faces shortfall. *The Dominion Post*, 4 November: 5.

Robson, Matt. 2001a. Land Information Easier: Information Technology Development: Survey and Titles Automation (Landonline). Quarterly Progress Report. Wellington: Office of the Minister for Land Information.

Robson, Matt. 2001b. Land Information New Zealand: Information Technology Development: Survey and Titles Automation (Landonline). Quarterly Progress Report. Wellington: Office of the Minister for Land Information.

Robson, Matt. 2001c Land Information New Zealand: Information Technology Development: Survey and Titles Automation (Landonline): Approval to Enter Contract for the Completion of Stage Two of Landonline. Wellington: Office of the Minister for Land Information.

Robson, Matt. 2002. Land Information New Zealand: Information Technology Development: Survey and Titles Automation (Landonline). Quarterly Progress Report. Wellington: Office of the Minister for Land Information.

Swain, Paul. 2000. Land Information New Zealand: Information Technology Development: Surveys and Titles Automation: Approval to Issue Tender Documents for the Design and Build of CRS2. Wellington: Office of the Minister for Land Information.

Tanner, Ross. 2003. Inquiry into the Requisition Rate for Survey Plans. Cranleigh Strategic Limited.

Teega Associates Ltd. 2003. Automation Program Evaluation. Wellington: LINZ.

Usherwood, B. 2001. Land Information New Zealand: Information Technology Development: Survey and Title Automation (Landonline). Progress Report for August 2001. Wellington: LINZ.

Yeabsley, John. 1997. External Benefits Revisited: Assessing the External Benefits of the Proposed LINZ Automation. Wellington: New Zealand Institute of Economic Research.

Chapter 7

Bain, Helen. 1996. Supercop on Top. *The Dominion*, 1 June: 18.

Cabinet Office. 2001. Monitoring Regimes for Major Information Technology (IT) Projects. Cabinet Office Circular CO (01) 4.

Chamberlain, Jenny. 1997. NZPD Blues: Can Cops Cope? *North and South*, October: 34–43.

Coddington, Deborah. 2001. Fair Cop: an interview with Greg O'Conner. *North and South*, August: 86–90.

Cohen, M.D., J.G. March, and J. Olsen. 1972. A garbage can theory of organizational choice. *Administrative Science Quarterly* 17: 1–25.

Computer World. 2004. MSD no on Swifft costs. *ComputerWorld*, Wednesday 2 June.

Davenport, T.H. 1996. Why reengineering failed: the fad that forgot people. *Fast Company, Premier Issue*: 70–4.

Doone, Peter. 1989. Potential Impacts of Community Policing on Criminal Investigation Strategies. In *Effectiveness and Change in Policing*, W. Young and N. Cameron (eds). Wellington: Institute of Criminology, Victoria University.

Doone, Peter. 1997. Letter to the Editor. *North and South*.

Galliers, R.D., and S. Newell. 2000. Back to the Future: From Knowledge Management to Data Management. Working Paper Series 92. London: LSE, Department of Information Systems.

Gregory, Robert. 1998. Country Report. A New Zealand Tragedy: Problems of Political Responsibility. *Governance* 11 (2): 231–40.

Hammer, M. 1990. Reeingineering Work: don't automate, obliterate. *Harvard Business Review*, July–August: 104–12.

Heeks, Richard. 2002. Failure, Success and Improvisation of Information System Projects in Developing Countries. Manchester: Institute for Development Policy and Management.

Hosking, Robert. 2002. ACC yet to explain its $173million IT blowout. *National Business Review*, 8 February: 10–11.

Luxton, John. 1995. Integrated National Crime Information System. Report to Cabinet State Sector Committee.

Macdonald, D. 2000. Governance and Oversight of Large Information Technology Projects. Wellington: Office of the Auditor-General.

Oakeshott, Michael Joseph. 1962. *Rationalism in politics, and other essays*. London: Methuen and Co.

SIMPL/NZIER. 2000. Information technology projects: Performance of the New Zealand public sector in performance. Report to the Department of the Prime Minister and Cabinet. Wellington: The SIMPL Group and New Zealand Institute of Economic Research (INC).

Small, Francis. 2000. Ministerial Inquiry into INCIS. Wellington.

State Services Commission (SSC). 1991. Review of Computing in the State Sector. Wellington: State Services Commission.

State Services Commission (SSC). 1992. *Getting the Bits Right*. Wellington: State Services Commission.

State Services Commission (SSC). 1997. Information Technology Stocktake. Wellington: State Services Commission.

State Services Commission (SSC). 2001. *Guidelines for Managing and Monitoring Major IT Projects*. State Services Commission and Treasury, August 2001. Available from http://www.ssc.govt.nz/documents/iguidelines/guidelines.html.

Teega Associates Ltd. 2003. Automation Program Evaluation. Wellington: LINZ.

Treasury, The. 2000. The Chief Executive Accountability Framework in the Budget Process as they Relate to Information Technology Projects. Wellington: Treasury.

Waitai, Rana (Chairperson). 1999. Inquiry into CARD and INCIS. Wellington: Justice and Law Reform Committee.

Index